ABOUT THE AUTHOR

Leslie Brandt has dedicated his life to the Lord and to the church as pastor, missionary, and writer.

After a missionary term in China, he served congregations in South Dakota, North Dakota, Minnesota, and California, and for three years he was a pastor to military personnel in Taiwan and Japan.

He has shared his personal faith, Bible knowledge, and pastoral experience in several bestselling books, including *Psalms/Now, Epistles/Now,* and *Meditations on a Loving God.* His *Book of Christian Prayer* has become a classic in its paper and gift editions. With his wife Edith he has also written *Growing Together,* a book of prayers for husbands and wives. He also is the author of another book in Augsburg's Bible Reading series, *Bible Readings for the Retired.*

Recently retired, Leslie Brandt now lives in Escondido, California, where he continues to write and serve area churches.

BIBLE READINGS SERIES

Bible Readings for Growing Christians
Kevin E. Ruffcorn

Bible Readings for Church Workers
Harry N. Huxhold

Bible Readings for Men
Steve Swanson

Bible Readings for the Retired
Leslie F. Brandt

Bible Readings for Couples
Margaret and Erling Wold

Bible Readings for Parents
Ron and Lyn Klug

Bible Readings for Teachers
Ruth Stenerson

Bible Readings for Singles
Ruth Stenerson

Bible Readings for Teenagers
Charles S. Mueller

Bible Readings for Families
Mildred and Luverne Tengbom

Bible Readings
FOR
TROUBLED
TIMES

Bible Readings

FOR TROUBLED TIMES

Leslie F. Brandt

AUGSBURG Publishing House • Minneapolis

BIBLE READINGS FOR TROUBLED TIMES

Copyright © 1984 Augsburg Publishing House

Library of Congress Cataloging in Publication Data

Brandt, Leslie F.
  BIBLE READINGS FOR TROUBLED TIMES.

  1. Bible—Meditations.   I. Title.
BS491.5.B73 1984   242'.5   84-18617
ISBN 0-8066-2130-3 (pbk.)

Manufactured in the U.S.A.   APH 10-0686

  2 3 4 5 6 7 8 9 0 1 2 3 4 5 6 7 8 9

PREFACE

C. S. Lewis prefaced his book *The Problem of Pain* by saying: "The only purpose of the book is to solve the intellectual problem raised by suffering; for the far higher task of teaching fortitude and patience I was never fool enough to suppose myself qualified, nor have anything to offer my readers except my conviction that when pain is to be borne, a little courage helps more than much knowledge, a little human sympathy more than much courage, and the least tincture of the love of God more than all."

This little volume falls far short of Lewis' purpose, which he handsomely fulfilled, but supports his conviction and endeavors to re-emphasize the "love of God" as that glorious factor we can all cling to when we face the troubles that come our way—and the pain that accompanies them.

I am unable to probe the dark depths of suffering felt by so many who have written so well. My pains and problems have been relatively small when compared to what they, and many who may read this volume, have experienced. Nevertheless, while I have no answers to the problem of pain, I believe in God's concern and love for his children despite the troubles that afflict their lives. I believe that our pain is God's pain as well, and he will bear it with us.

■ THE DIVINE ENCOUNTER

Exod. 3:13-17:   "I am who I am" (v. 14).

I am who I am." This is about as much as human thought can manage in defining God. It was enough for Moses—especially when it was followed by the promise to bring him and his people "out of your misery in Egypt into the land of the Canaanites." God revealed himself more clearly in his Son, Jesus Christ, and then extended his promise to deliver all of his children from the consequences of sin and eternal death.

Through the God who spoke to Moses and the Christ whom he sent into our world, we have encountered the divine—our Creator, Redeemer, and King. When we are troubled and afflicted, we are such as God's beloved children. This divine encounter has resulted in faith, the God-gifted ability to believe that he who delivered Israel out of their afflictions in Egypt will deliver us.

God has, through the cross and resurrection of Jesus Christ, delivered us from sin and death and its eternal consequences. But he has not delivered us out of all the troubles that have come our way. They will continue to plague us, frighten us, confound us. Yet those of us who have encountered the Divine can be assured that he lovingly abides with us and he goes with us in and through our sufferings.

 I thank you, my God, for encountering me through the Word and the sacraments, and for staying close to me amidst life's uncountable troubles.

Where in your daily life do you encounter God?

9

■ WHY WAS I EVER BORN?

Job 3:1-16: "May the day of my birth perish . . ."
(v. 3).

W hy then did you bring me out of the womb? I
wish I had died before any eye saw me" (Job 10:18).
Job's brash and almost sacrilegious attitude toward
life is no longer strange to most of us. We have all
questioned God about our existence. It may have
begun in childhood when our parents refused to
grant us something we wanted very much. There
have been occasions since when the question has been
more sincere and often desperate: "Why was I ever
born?"

The apostle Paul has an answer: "For he chose us
in him before the creation of the world to be holy and
blameless in his sight. In love he predestined us to be
adopted as his sons [and daughters] through Jesus
Christ" (Eph. 1:4-5). We are precious in God's sight,
each one of us individually so important to him that
he went to the cross to save us from our sins.

We are, nevertheless, born to be human. And in a
world full of troubles and where evil forces are
increasingly active, we will be plagued with problems
and pain. "A righteous man may have many troubles,"
wrote the psalmist, "but the Lord delivers him from
them all" (Ps. 34:19). That deliverance may be a long
time in coming, but come it will, because we are God's
beloved children.

 I celebrate your acceptance of me as your
child and servant, O Lord. Grant that I be faithful
to you.

**Have you ever felt like Job? Recall how God
delivered you.**

■ NEXT IN LINE

Job 4:1-6: "Now it's your turn to be in trouble" (v. 5 TEV).

We sometimes treat the troubles of others in a light-hearted manner—secretly relieved that they didn't happen to us. Then it's our turn to be in trouble, and we wonder why others appear to be so unconcerned. But when we have learned to cope with our troubles, we may develop a more sympathetic and understanding attitude toward others who are in pain.

Job's friend, Eliphaz, credited Job for being kind and helpful to others in trouble. "Now," he said to Job, "it's your turn to be in trouble, and you are too stunned to face it." Some of us have led rather sheltered lives in our younger years, little realizing the appalling suffering that is going on in the world about us. The day comes when some tragedy or breakdown, illness or accident, some ugly rupture takes place with us or those closely associated with us, "and we are too stunned to face it."

First there is shock, then anger, followed by grief. Through it all there is hope for the Christian, and with hope comes solace and comfort and strength. We often fail God; he never fails us. He will not when it is our turn to face trouble.

 My troubles often obscure you, my God, and my faith is weak. I am grateful that this does not separate me from you.

Think of ways in which your troubles have made you more sympathetic toward others.

■ THE HUMAN CONDITION

Job 14:1-6: "We are all born weak and helpless. All lead the same short, troubled life" (v. 1 TEV).

Job is speaking about the dark side of humanity. He is deeply depressed as the result of the hideous happenings in his life. Yet his words are remarkably accurate in respect to the human condition. They are similar to Paul's words: "There is no one righteous . . . all have turned away . . . become worthless . . . no one who does good . . . all have sinned and fall short of the glory of God" (Rom. 3:10-24).

This is indeed the human condition, and from it issue most of the troubles that beset us. "We are all born weak and helpless . . . and lead the same, short troubled life." Paul, however, writes words that Job could not utter, and brings light and hope to this dark scene: "Since we have been justified by faith, we have peace with God through our Lord Jesus Christ" (Rom. 5:1).

These are the words that apply to each of us regardless of the troubles that pursue us. While they do not give clear answers to all our troubles or may not immediately lessen the pain that afflicts us, they diminish their importance with the blazing hope of love and peace and joy—and the ultimate end to all human troubles in a redeemed and eternal relationship with God. "Thanks be to God—through Jesus Christ our Lord!" (Rom. 7:25).

 I thank you, my God, that my weaknesses and helplessness do not deter your love for me nor destroy my relationship with you.

Copy Rom. 5:1 on a card and place it where it can remind you of your relationship with God.

■ DEALING WITH DESPAIR

Job 23:1-12: "If only I knew where to find him"
(v. 3).

A prison inmate in England escaped the confines of
his cell. After several days of searching, the officials
found him huddled in a chimney on the prison roof.
There he was, just his head and shoulders sticking out,
shouting plaintively, "Nobody loves me."

Loneliness may well be the most excruciating of all
agonies, and the condition most likely to lead to
despair. It might have been loneliness that provoked
the psalmist to cry out: "Save me, O God, for the
waters have come up to my neck" (Ps. 69:1). He was
in despair, and there are times when we can identify
with him.

It was probably Job's loneliness that produced
despair in his life. His friends simply compounded
his misery by their self-righteous indictments. God
himself seemed totally out of reach.

Through Jesus Christ, our God is ever within reach.
He has found us and will never forsake us. The
Scriptures declare his love for us. "For everything that
was written in the past was written to teach us,
so that through endurance and the encouragement
of the Scriptures we might have hope" (Rom. 15:4).

Because of the Word and the sacrament and the
friends who will love us if we give them the
opportunity, we need not harbor the demon of
despair. We need only return to the Source of love
and joy, our Lord Jesus Christ.

 I praise you, my God, for though I could not find
you, you have found me and will always know
where I am.

**Memorize today's prayer and repeat it when you are
tempted to despair.**

■ WHEN YOU ARE BITTER

Job 27:1-6: "... the Almighty, who has made me taste bitterness of soul" (v. 2).

The farther I journey in life—God help me—the less comfort I find," said St. Teresa of Avila. While some of God's children appear to be soaring in joy, victorious over all their troubles, others of us feel that the road before us becomes narrower and rougher as we grow older. There are times when we can understand what Job felt in the dark, unfathomable depths of his life. While we do not blame the Almighty for our state of mind, we confess to feelings of bitterness. Life is short; our pains severe; our conflicts fierce; our demons vicious.

We find little comfort in this portion of Job's response to his suffering. But we find much to strengthen and sustain us in the lives of Christ and his faithful followers. We discover that God accepts us even in our bitterness. God even feels something of the pain that forces us into these dark periods of life.

If our bitterness is not confronted and dealt with, it may destroy us. God's grace is promised and available to keep that from happening to any of us. It is time to pray as Jesus prayed: "Father, into your hands I commit my spirit." If that prayer is genuine and our lives truly placed in God's hands, the miracle of divine grace will take over.

 I commit these terrible feelings of bitterness into your hands, O God. Overcome them and fill me with the joy of being your child whatever the sufferings I must embrace in the journey before me.

Are there any feelings of bitterness in your life? Today confess them and turn them over to God.

■ WE ARE SECURE

Psalm 3: "You are a shield around me, O Lord" (v. 3).

There are times in our lives when we are inclined to pass off the psalmist's claim as wishful thinking. Yet the psalm writers repeated this theme again and again —usually in the midst of their fears and doubts and woeful complaints.

While the psalmist appears to be a complex of contradictions in these sometimes despondent, sometimes joyous songs of his faith, he reaches for a far deeper and often incomprehensible truth that stands above and beyond the adversities that so often harassed him. Despite the onslaughts of his enemies and the many troubles that afflict him, he is secure in the belief that his God is a shield about him.

This is the witness of countless scores of saints from that time until this. They often endured the fires of adversity and the pains of persecution only to leave in their wake joyous songs of confidence in their loving God who accompanied them and secured them amidst their dire sufferings.

Our great God does not secure us against troubles. God does promise to keep us secure in their midst and assures us that the troubles and tragedies that beset our world and its inhabitants will not come between us and his eternal love.

 Help me never to forget, dear God, that whatever the tribulations of this life, I am forever secure in you.

Several times today repeat Ps. 3:3: "You are a shield around me, O Lord."

■ RELIEF FOR THE DISTRESSED

Psalm 4: "Give me relief from my distress" (v. 1).

Some of the troubles that come our way are the consequences of our own careless activities, but many of the disagreeable things that happen to us are not our direct responsibility. We can't understand why we are expected to deal with them. Neither does the psalmist understand, nor does he pretend that they don't exist. He meets them, accepts them, and rises above them with assurance and joy.

We simply cannot ignore these troubles for long. We can't wish them out of existence or suppose them to be illusions. We can't run away from them. We must face them. But we don't have to face them alone. There is relief for our children when they are in trouble—in our hearts and homes. There is relief from the heart of God for his distressed and despairing sons and daughters. It may be through the institutions that concerned people have set up, or through loving friends within calling distance. Through his servants who live to serve, through the Scriptures, prayer, the writings of others who have endured the storm before us, God offers relief for those in distress.

"Come to me, all you who are weary and burdened, and I will give you rest," said our Lord (Matt. 11:28) —and he means it.

 I am eternally grateful, my Lord, because I can always find rest and relief in your love for me.

Where can you go to receive God's help in your distress?

■ WHEN DEPRESSION SETS IN

Psalm 6:   "My soul is in anguish. How long, O Lord, how long?" (v. 3).

There are many things to be depressed about: personal wrongdoings, errors, loneliness, ill health, unemployment, financial insecurity, broken relationships, the conditions of the world. Then there are times when we are depressed for no identifiable reason. Drugs can grant temporary relief, but the problem remains unsolved and only worsens as one becomes dependent on pills or powders or liquid spirits for the courage to face each day.

It takes courage to accept the things that we cannot change as well as to work on those things that can be changed. Much depends on the direction of our daily intent or focus. If it is earthward, we find little purpose or power that will enable us to confront and deal with such matters. If, like the psalmist, our focus is on God and our trust in his love and will for our lives, we are in touch with divine promises and purposes, and our depression can be handled by a determination to plod onward irrespective of those dark feelings that often obscure the road before us.

"The Lord has heard my cry for mercy; the Lord accepts my prayer," wrote the psalmist. He was convinced that the sun would ultimately break through the cloud cover. As it did for him, it will for us.

 My focus is on you, my Lord. Enable me to feel something of your love for me today.

When you feel depressed, focus on God and his love for you.

■ WHEN TROUBLES WON'T GO AWAY

Psalm 10:   "Why do you hide yourself in times of trouble?" (v. 1).

Why did this happen to me? we ask. *Why was I ever born? Why do I have to suffer while others are healthy and happy?*

Sometimes we ask these questions because we believe that everything happens by God's direction and will. Perhaps we have forgotten the risks and the joys, the pains and the possibilities of the gift of freedom that our Creator so lovingly imparted to us. To be free means to be removed from God's absolute and total manipulation so we can make choices, live and work in loving relationships with God and with other people.

Such freedom is both beautiful and terrible, joyful and sorrowful, precious and awesome. We can choose to live as God's children (by his grace through Christ's redeeming love), or through self-worship and self-gratification to become the instruments of evil. We can choose to love or hate, live or die. God, in his wisdom, gave us this gift, this freedom, because it was the only way that we could become his true sons and daughters.

It means, however, that we are subject to the pains of being human in our world, that God cannot or will not shield us from the tragic hours of life. Our question should not be, "why?" It should be, "What do I do now that this has happened to me?"

 I accept the pain, O God. Now grant me the grace to deal with it.

In place of the question, "Why, Lord?" ask: "Lord, what do you want me to do about this?"

18

■ THE PAIN THAT PERSISTS

Psalm 13:   "How long must I wrestle with my
thoughts . . . and have sorrow in my heart?" (v. 2).

Suffering and pain do not come to us as willed by
God. These pains and sorrows happen to us because
we are human. We will continue to mourn the loss of
loved ones, because disease harms and destroys. We
lose beloved friends because of fire or flood or
earthquakes or drunk drivers. We may at any time lose
our health to a debilitating illness or our lives to some
stupid accident.

In *When Bad Things Happen to Good People*
Harold Kushner insists that God has limitations, that
"he is limited in what he can do by laws of nature and
by the evolution of human nature and human moral
freedom . . . he neither causes nor prevents tragedies."

While we affirm Kushner's assertion that God does
not *cause* calamities and tragedies, we question his
conviction that God cannot *prevent* them. And this is
in the light of the frequent miraculous deliverances
and healings in the New Testament, as well as those
some of us have experienced or witnessed
throughout our lives.

But what about the Holocaust and Jonestown and
the hundreds of millions throughout our world who
have suffered so horribly? We do not have a clear
answer that explains why God did not intervene to
prevent such horrendous events from happening.

 O Lord, I cannot understand why bad things
should happen to me. Give strength to my
sagging faith that I may trust you even without
explanations.

Today affirm Ps. 13:5: "I trust in your unfailing love."

■ WILL GOD INTERVENE?

Ps. 18:1-19:   "He rescued me because he delighted in me" (v. 19).

It appears that God did intervene in David's crisis, and rescued him from the hands of his enemies as well as the wrath of King Saul. When things went their way, the Old Testament leaders assumed that it was because God acted on their behalf. God received the credit and the psalmists sang his praises.

When good things happen in our lives we should by all means speak and sing our grateful praises to him.

But there are also periods of pain and suffering when God appears to be indifferent to our cries for help. What about those times? Do they mean that God does not "delight" in us?

Perhaps there are times when God cannot intervene in our lives to rescue us from the troubles that crowd around us. Instead, we are to confront and deal with them with the grace that he confers upon us. Does he nonetheless delight in us? We know the answer to that question: God does indeed delight in the love and faith of his children. We have already been delivered from sin and its eternal consequences, and there is no trouble or tragedy that can cancel out that great deliverance.

 My God, I cannot understand how you can still delight in me. Yet I praise you for my deliverance from sin and trust you to keep me through the trials from which I am not delivered.

In the midst of your troubles remind yourself that God continues to delight in you.

■ WHEN YOU FEEL ABANDONED

Ps. 22:1-11:   "My God, my God, why have you abandoned me?" (v. 1 TEV).

These were the very words Jesus cried out in the midst of his excruciating pain and loneliness. Like Job of old, like most of us at times in our lives, even Jesus asked, "Why, O God, why?" God did not put Jesus on the cross; the hands of Roman soldiers and the raucous cries of his own people put him there. Our Lord did not want to suffer; it was the inevitable consequence of living and working as the Son of God in this world. Yet it was God who turned that event into the means of our redemption.

Jesus' feelings of abandonment during his dying on the cross were soon to be followed by his glorious resurrection. This is the living hope of all of God's sons and daughters. Our ultimate deliverance is assured. The prelude to that deliverance will include the minor chords of pain and loneliness and abandonment. But we know that God never abandoned Christ, nor does he abandon any of us.

Pain is a part of the price of living in this world to which God has entrusted us. It is integral to the human condition. Dare we embrace it, knowing that God is with us to enable us to bear it and that it will not last forever? Dare we believe that though God does not inflict us with these agonizing hours of pain and loneliness, he can use them to work out his purpose in our lives?

I sometimes feel abandoned, Lord, but your Word constantly assures me of your faithfulness. May that Word and your promises bring peace to my aching heart.

Find an Easter picture that can remind you of God's ultimate deliverance.

■ SHADOWS

Psalm 23:   "Even though I walk through the valley of the shadow of death . . ." (v. 4).

We are indeed "walking through the valley of the shadow." Every day we die a little. "A little while and I will be gone from among you, whither I cannot tell," were among the last words of an Indian chief. "From nowhere we come, into nowhere we go. What is life? It is a flash of a firefly in the night. It is a breath of a buffalo in the winter time. It is as the little shadow that runs across the grass and loses itself in the sunset." Whether or not God may shield us from some of the troubles and tragedies that we encounter, we know that he will not shield us from the ultimate event —death.

It is not, however, an event that we need fear. "For you are with me," sang the psalmist. "Your rod and your staff, they comfort me." Some of the troubles that we face—a serious illness, a dangerous mission, the threat of a nuclear holocaust—are "shadows" that haunts us in our valley sojourn. There lurks behind them that final, sometimes ominous, always disquieting shadow of death. The resurrection of Jesus Christ removes that shadow and cancels out all foreboding in respect to death. "We fear no evil; for you are with us." God can not prevent us from going through the event, but he will be there to meet and accompany us.

 My Lord, I cannot be certain how I will react to the threat of death when it comes, but I believe that your grace will be sufficient even in that last hour of my life.

Try memorizing all of Psalm 23.

■ AFRAID OF THE DARK

Psalm 27: "The Lord is my light and my salvation—whom shall I fear?" (v. 1).

The unknown future is dark and obscure to us. The journey ahead is fraught with danger. Our planet is not as secure as we once thought it to be. Some of us take life one day at a time because we are afraid of tomorrow. The characteristic of our age is uncertainty.

The psalmist poses some brave statements and questions: "The Lord is my light and salvation . . . the stronghold of my life . . . of whom shall I be afraid?" We are not as convinced as he appears to be that "in the day of trouble he will keep us safe in his dwelling," or "hide us in the shelter of his tabernacle." There have been and will be those times when we have not been and will not be sheltered from the ravages of wind and water, from people's evil deeds or nature's devastating powers.

Yet the proclamations of the psalmist are absolutely true: "The Lord *is* our light and salvation . . . the stronghold of our lives," and this most certainly ought to shore up our hearts with courage. We must be careful lest we bring on our own troubles, but we need not be fearful in the face of calamities and troubles that befall us in our world. We can take heart and wait for the Lord, for he is our light and salvation.

 O God, the future is so loaded with fearful questions and events, and my faith so often wavers. You have stayed with me through the past; grant me the courage to face whatever lies ahead.

Affirm many times today: "The Lord is my light and my salvation."

■ IN THE HANDS OF GOD

Psalm 31: "My times are in your hands" (v. 15).

The psalmist was railing against his trouble-fraught existence, suffering in his loneliness, groping desperately for a way out. He asked "why" and received no answer. "Save me, O God, for the waters have come up to my neck," he once cried (Ps. 69:1). Job despised his birth. Paul wrote: "What a wretched man I am! Who will rescue me from this body of death?" (Rom. 7:24). It was in the midst of his fearful and heart-wrenching experiences that the psalmist found the key to coping. It is articulated in his classic statement: "My times are in your hands."

It appears to be something of a paradox—that we can go through hell-like miseries and still be in the hands of God. The psalmist believed it; Job experienced it and finally declared it. The apostle Paul discovered it to be true in his life (Rom. 8:25). Maybe even Jesus had some nagging doubts about his life and ministry in his last hours on earth as his very disciples betrayed him or ran away in fear when the crowds screamed, "Crucify him" and Roman soldiers executed him. Yet his very last words on the cross were: "Father, into your hands I commit my spirit" (Luke 23:46).

This is indeed our key to coping. The way to face future problems, or to handle the pain and grief of past and present days, is to commit our spirits, our lives, our times into the hands of God.

My times are in your hands, my God. Now help me to believe it and to act upon it.

Clip a picture of hands from a magazine. Place it where it can remind you that your life is in God's good hands.

■ OUR TROUBLE WITH GUILT

Psalm 32: "Blessed is he whose transgressions are forgiven, whose sins are covered" (v. 1).

Job's friends meant well, but did more to aggravate his sufferings than to diminish them. They felt it was their moral duty to convince Job that the reason for his suffering was guilt and sin in his life. Job refused to accept their judgments upon him.

One thing we learn from the story of Job is that suffering is not God's intended punishment for failure or wrongdoing. Nevertheless, feelings of guilt do play a prominent role in much of the suffering that afflict God's children. Guilt feelings are sometimes necessary to spiritual growth, but if they unnecessarily persist, they may cause mental or physical illness.

Perhaps the psalmist discovered this for himself and thus stressed the vital importance of forgiveness. Is it possible that some of the troubles we confront have their basis in guilt feelings? If so, there is a remedy that offers the way to deal with them. "I said, 'I will confess my transgressions to the Lord'—and you forgave the guilt of my sin" (v. 5). "Blessed is he whose transgressions are forgiven, whose sins are covered."

The cure for guilt is forgiveness of sin. It was made possible at a great price—the blood of Jesus Christ. We have been set free, forgiven, and accepted by the love of God. Believe it! It is true!

 I believe it, Lord. I believe it. I cannot comprehend it, but I believe it. You have forgiven me, and my iniquities will not be held against me.

Write the sins that bother you on a piece of paper. Then destroy it as a sign that God has forgiven you.

■ WHEN WE CAN'T DO IT ALONE

Ps. 35:1-10: "Contend, O Lord, with those who contend with me" (v. 1).

The psalmist was aware that God could not or would not eliminate the demons within him or the enemies around him. Living in this world means living with enemies, troubles, pain. This is the price of freedom —the precious gift that God gave to his human creatures. God does not make robots; God makes people—free to love and serve him, free to make up their own gods and serve them, and free to contend with the forces of evil and those whom such forces control. Among other things, this means that we have to live with troubles—some that we can't handle by ourselves.

God has promised our ultimate deliverance from all that hurts and causes fear, but God's present intervention in our problems is seldom miraculous—at least in the way we think of miracles. God usually works in our lives through other human beings and institutions. The hands of God that reach out to heal are the human hands of his creatures who are gifted and trained to help and heal us in our troubles, or to bear us up in our brokenness.

God does contend with us against the sufferings, the troubles, the evil forces that are the enemies of our souls. We need never be ashamed to seek his help. He knows the enemy; he suffers with his children as they experience the traumas of living in a chaotic world.

 O God, I need your help with this problem that I face; I cannot handle it on my own. Work out your will in and through me.

Thank God for the people and institutions that are the channels for his help to you.

■ TALKING OURSELVES OUT OF TROUBLE

Psalm 42:   "Why are you downcast, O my soul?" (v. 11).

Depression or despondency is a very real thing even if we don't know the cause or the reason for it. It may be that the psalmist, after discovering that God did not shield him from all the unhappy circumstances of life, was learning how to deal with despondency by talking himself out of it. He acknowledges his soul-thirst for God and his faith in God—and this despite the ridicule of his adversaries. He remembers his past experiences, particularly those that had to do with the joy of worshiping with others in the house of God.

It is not simple, but sometimes it is possible to talk ourselves out of our little caves of despondency. The God we rejoiced in with others in those sanctuaries of our past and who was so real to us in those times is fully as present with us today. We may not *feel* his presence in the same way we did then, and life may appear more distressful and uncertain to us now than it did in our youth. God, however, has not changed, nor have his precious promises. We are as much his beloved children and servants now as we have ever been.

Let us begin talking with ourselves about these troubles that waylay us. They may become less threatening and our relationship to God more secure as we meditate upon his everlasting love for us.

 Enable me, my great God, to overcome my fickle feelings and really trust you. Help me to sense your eternal love for me.

Read Psalms 42 and 43, paying attention to how the psalmist talks his way out of despondency.

■ AN EVER PRESENT HELP

Psalm 46: "God is our refuge and strength, an ever present help in trouble" (v. 1).

God does not send viruses that shorten our lives. God does not punish his creatures by wiping out whole populations with war or plague or terrorist bombs. He is not responsible for the nuclear-arms buildup that threatens the total destruction of our planet. Apart from the natural disasters which randomly cause much suffering and loss of life at times, much of this earth's tragedies are caused by the greed and lust for power and the carelessness and sickness of the human race.

We know that our troubles are not sent by God, but are the consequence and price of living in this world and of being members of the human race. It is necessary that we recognize that the troubles that trip us up are not of God's choosing and may not be eliminated by our praying.

God has declared it—as did the psalmist—and we can believe it, that our loving God is "an ever present help in trouble." It is, however, *in* trouble that he is "our refuge and strength" and, miracle of miracles, *through* trouble that he often works out his will and purposes in and through us.

 I need to feel and believe as did the psalmist, that you are an ever present help in trouble, dear Lord. Respond to the need for help in my life, O my Savior.

Make a small poster or banner with the words of Ps. 46:1.

■ WHAT WE HAVE GOING FOR US

Ps. 68:1-20: "Praise to the Lord, to God our Savior, who daily bears our burdens" (v. 19).

We live in an uncertain and insecure world. Our relationship to this world and its inhabitants is equally tenuous. Some things we can be certain of are the troubles, the hurts, the sufferings and conflicts that assail us along our way. The psalmist was looking to the mighty acts of God as revealed in nature to comfort him on his daily course through life. We are able to look to God's internal presence through the gifts of his Spirit to succor and sustain us day by day.

If only we would believe it—that the same power that brought the visible Christ into our world by way of the womb of the virgin Mary and raised him from the dead on the day of resurrection is the same power, that divine energy, that abides in us.

How dare we act as if our great God is too small to bear us up in the face of our comparatively small troubles, to enable us to confront and cope with the problems that badger us from one day to the next? We must rise up in faith rather than grovel in our miseries, recognize who we are and what we have become through Christ, and accept each day, whatever it may bring us, with courage and confidence. The Lord is blessed indeed, and he "daily bears our burdens."

> Forgive me, dear Lord, for groveling in my miseries when I could be grappling with life and circumstances in the power of your Spirit. I have so much to learn. Be patient with me. Continue to bear me up as you teach me how to live victoriously in the midst of human conflicts and sorrows.

Remember each day that God is helping to bear your burdens.

■ LIVING AFTER LOSING

Ps. 69:1-15: "For the waters have come up to my neck . . . the floods engulf me" (vv. 1-2).

One can hardly imagine a grief-stricken situation that is more excruciating than that described by the author of this psalm. "I am worn out calling for help; my throat is parched. My eyes fail, looking for my God." The cries are not from a man in physical pain, or even a terminally ill person approaching death. It is even more agonizing and debilitating than that.

It may be likened to a mother whose child was killed by a drunken driver or a husband who lost his wife through a consuming disease. Someone has lost the most treasured person in his life, and there is apparently nothing that can cushion the mental and emotional anguish of this horrible, irreplaceable loss.

What can we do if it happens to us? How can we go on living after such a loss? We cry out in anger to God—until we realize that he is not responsible for drunk drivers or destructive illnesses. Does it help if we can accept God as a grieving God because he is a loving God, who feels something of the pain that we feel? Are we able to find some comfort in his love for us and the assurance that he is close beside us when we "sink in the miry depths where there is no foothold . . . and the waters come up to our necks?" The psalmist apparently did so, for even this psalm turned into a song of praise and faith. It will take time, and the memory will always cause us pain, but the love of God will also comfort and assure us.

 You know my anguish, O Lord. Grant me your comfort, and the strength to live with it and eventually to overcome it.

Read the rest of Psalm 69 and see how the psalmist is moved to faith and praise.

■ THE MATTER OF FAILURE

Psalm 73: "My flesh and my heart may fail, but God is the strength of my heart" (v. 26).

Some of us find failure—moral or spiritual—in marriage, business, interpersonal relationships, to be a heart-wrenching experience. While we admit to being finite and fallible creatures, we find it difficult to accept imperfections. What we find almost impossible to comprehend is that it is our flaws and deficiencies that make us eligible for God's loving grace and forgiveness.

The psalmist accepted the fact of failure. The apostle Paul wrote: "What a wretched man I am!" "I am unclean," the leper admitted to Christ, and it was one of the prerequisites for being made clean. "I am unworthy," confessed the centurion, and it was the beginning of a great miracle in his life.

There are no successes without failures. As troublesome as they are, failures may be the threshold to success. Failure slays self-sufficiency and prepares us for faith. Faith in the grace and power of God through Christ will not necessarily bring success as the world interprets it, but will result in making us effectual as his children and servants. Regardless of our failures, "Never will I leave you; never will I forsake you," says our Lord (Heb. 13:5). It is a promise that we can count on and live by.

 Eternal God, I acknowledge my failures even as I lay claim to your forgiving love. Keep them from hurting anyone else today.

What have been the major failures in your life? Admit them today and accept God's forgiveness.

■ DEALING WITH SOLITUDE

Psalm 71: "Do not cast me away when I am old; do not forsake me when my strength is gone" (v. 9).

Christopher Fry has written: "No man is free who will not dare to pursue the questions of his own loneliness. It is through them that he lives." The greatest loneliness may be felt when the children leave home, or when we lose our mate, or a dear friend leaves our circle of love. After the death of her husband, Ardis Whitman discovered that "solitude is a part of the inescapable enterprise of maturing . . . it never leaves you the same . . . you emerge from it angrier or gentler, sterner or more compassionate, more bitter or more loving, more shut up or more communicating, but never the same."

Whatever the reason or cause for our solitariness, we should learn how to handle it. We need to be sure of God's love and care when nobody is around to affirm it and assure us of it.

This is often a painful experience, but it need not be depressing. We will possibly discover, even in our hours of solitude, the kind of joy and peace that we never realized in the noisy and busy years of our lives. One thing is certain: God will never cast us away, or forsake us when our strength is gone. We are never really alone, and when we lovingly reach out to others, we will eventually touch somebody who is reaching out to us.

 I am reaching out for you, O God. Help me to sense your presence in these hours of solitude and to know something of that peace and joy that come only from you.

Choose a prayer from those at the end of this book.

■ THE NEED TO BE RESTORED

Psalm 85:   "Restore us again, O God our Savior"
(v. 4).

If our failures continue to trouble us, this may point up our need for restoration to God and his purposes for our lives. Failures do not stand in the way of our salvation, because our salvation is not the consequence of our works, but is the gift of God's grace through Jesus Christ. "For it is by grace you have been saved, through faith," wrote Paul, "and this not from yourselves, it is the gift of God" (Eph. 2:8). There are times, however, when we need to be restored to that joy and peace that God grants through his gift of salvation.

We may be in need of a second conversion. We need to recognize anew God's saving love and our responsibilities as his children and servants. Because we so often fail, we often need to rededicate or recommit ourselves to his plan for our lives. We are truly the sons and daughters of God, yet we frequently revert to self-centered thoughts and actions, attempting to run our own lives and serve our own interests. Our response to God's saving grace is to give his will priority in our daily affairs and to faithfully serve him by loving and serving our neighbor.

If this is our decision and determination, God will hold our failures as of little account and lovingly restore us to himself.

 I feel, O Lord, that you are so far away. I do not have your peace in my life. Restore to me the joy of that salvation you have won for me.

Whenever your failures or troubles cause you to doubt, ask God to restore the joy of your salvation.

■ FEELING SORRY FOR YOURSELF

Psalm 90: "The length of our days is seventy years
. . . yet their span is but trouble and sorrow" (v. 10).

Feeling sorry for ourselves does us more harm than
do most of the troubles that clutter up our lives. We
tend to brood over the past—as if things were so much
better back there. We create rifts between ourselves
and others and make them feel uncomfortable by our
presence. We accentuate the negative aspects that are
present in the human condition. We live by our fickle
feelings that change with the weather and often have
little to do with the facts of life.

We can do very little about the troubles we face
until we meet head-on with things as they really are.
This includes the truths that God does not put
troubles in our way, that we are his beloved children
forever, that our God abides with us in the midst of all
our difficult circumstances and is able to accomplish
his purposes in our lives in spite of or through such
circumstances.

This day may be the last day of our lives, our final
time on this earth to laugh and play or complete some
unfinished task, right a wrong, fulfill an obligation,
or to touch someone with love. It would be a shame to
waste it on self-pity.

 Forgive me, O God, for crawling in self-pity
when I should be serving you and my fellow
persons in joy. Enable me to demonstrate your
resurrection power in my life.

**What can you do today to complete a task or reach
out to someone else in love?**

■ SALVATION WITH SUFFERING

Psalm 91:   "I will be with him in trouble, I will deliver him . . . and show him my salvation" (vv. 15-16).

The psalmist is optimistic about God's care for his children in times of trouble. He even appears to be unrealistic when he says that no harm or disaster will come near us. He knows better, and so do we. Harm does befall us; disasters do come near; and angels do not always keep us from dashing our feet against stones.

What the psalm writer may be attempting to do in this beautiful song is to assure us that God will be with us in our troubles, that such do not come between us and his love. "Your Father . . . causes his sun to rise on the evil and the good, and sends rain on the righteous and on the unrighteous," said Jesus (Matt. 5:45), and while our troubles and sufferings do not come from God, they afflict all of his children as well as those who do not recognize him as God of their lives.

Deliverance will ultimately come to those who love God. "I will rescue them," says the Lord. In the meantime, the psalmist assures us that God will be with us in trouble. He will deliver us and honor us and show us his salvation.

 I thank you, my loving God, for your precious promises that keep me secure regardless of the terrors of the night and the pestilence that stalks in darkness. Grant to me the courage and grace to combat these troublesome things in my life.

Today affirm: "God is with me in trouble. God will deliver me."

■ GROWING PAINS

Psalm 94: "Blessed is the man you discipline, O Lord" (v. 12).

The biblical writers often regarded the calamities that happened to the Israelites as the chastisement of God upon them. In fact, they credited God for almost everything that happened to them—good or bad. This is a simplistic and inadequate approach to the troubles and misfortunes that plague humanity, but is still in some measure accepted by some Christians today.

This approach doesn't do much for us. It certainly does nothing to eliminate our conflicts or to make us feel better in the midst of our troubles. On the other hand, most of us probably agree that troubles and sufferings that have assailed us have, in fact, served as a disciplining that nudged us back into a closer relationship to God. Even though such sufferings were not sent by God, they may have enabled us to see the transitoriness of life on this planet or the foolishness of investing too heavily in earthly treasures.

"Those whom I love, I rebuke and discipline," said our Lord (Rev. 3:19). We may consider the effects of some of the troubles we face as a disciplining, because the pains we endure may be the "growing pains" that mature our lives in the Christian faith. This could be the reason for Paul's statement: "We rejoice in our sufferings, because we know that suffering produces perseverance" (Rom. 5:3).

 If the result of my sufferings resolve in a closer relationship with you, my Lord, I rejoice in them.

Can you recall a time when troubles have led you closer to God?

◼ WE ARE SIGNIFICANT

Psalm 100:   ''We are his people, the sheep of his pasture'' (v. 3).

One of the problems that affects people, and is capable of causing trouble in their lives, is their inability to recognize and accept their own validity and significance. A contemporary writer once prayed: "Give me some measure of success, O God, some sense of importance, some mountain on which to be transfigured, some out-of-this-world experience to give wings to my flagging spirit." The prayer was never answered, nor does it need to be. We *are* important; we *are* significant. "How great is the love the Father has lavished on us, that we should be called children of God! And that is what we are!" wrote John (1 John 3:1).

We are significant! It's an eternal truth declared and constantly reiterated by God's Word that no ugliness or failure, sin or defeat can nullify. Whatever our past upbringing or present circumstances, our weaknesses or distortions, or the troubles that confront us in this moment, we are important—because "we are his people, the sheep of his pasture."

This remarkable and eternal truth can take the fear and frustration out of the troubles we face and give us the courage to charge into them like the lions of God. It may not eliminate the pain or the suffering that befalls us in our trouble-fraught lives, but it will give us the strength to endure, for God made us his people, his own to love forever.

 I thank you, O God, for making me significant, for putting meaning and purpose into my life, for adopting me into your family.

Remind yourself today: "As God's child I am significant."

■ SURROUNDED BY THE LOVE OF GOD

Psalm 125: "As the mountains surround Jerusalem, so the Lord surrounds his people" (v. 2).

We will find little comfort in this song and analogy of the psalmist if we assume that "the mountains" around us will thereby make us immune to the pain and sufferings, the conflicts and defeats, the frustrations and aggravations that afflict all of us at times. Even those mountains round about Jerusalem were frequently breached by Israel's enemies. Probably no people had as many troubles or suffered so severely as did the children of Israel throughout the centuries. Yet they were in an amazing and miraculous way surrounded by the love of God.

Thus it is with us. God does not send or wish upon us these troubles. They are the plight of every human creature on this sin-ridden planet. Nor does God promise to shield us from trouble in this world. Nevertheless, "we are his people, the sheep of his pasture" (Ps. 100). It certainly means that he is with us, knows our suffering and pain, and embraces and encompasses us with his love. Even in the midst of the many negatives of this life, we are indeed surrounded by God's love and concern, secure in our relationship to him. He promises that his children who "sow in tears will reap with songs of joy" (Ps. 126:5).

 Gracious heavenly Father, grant to me the faith to believe that I am encompassed by your love, and courage to live in spite of and even in the midst of things I cannot change.

Consider the many positive things in your life, made possible by God's abiding love.

■ THE GIFT OF FORGIVENESS

Psalm 130: "If you, O Lord, kept a record of sins, O Lord, who could stand?" (v. 3).

The song of the psalmist registers a searing question —one that can be the basis for deep troubles in people's lives. The psalmist, however, gives the comforting, life-giving message: "But with you there is forgiveness." God's gift of forgiveness, as revealed through the cross of Jesus Christ, does not eliminate all of the consequences of our iniquitous deeds and mistakes, but wipes out their guilt and restores us to our loving God.

This redemptive restoration to God is the cure for the most serious troubles of our lives and becomes a basis for dealing with hurts and sorrows we have brought upon ourselves and others. It will not immediately solve all of our problems, but it is a necessary beginning.

We need only return to the cross of Christ and there claim anew the forgiving grace and love of God. As we leave our sins there, many of our troubles will be left with them, and we like the psalmist, can go on to thanksgiving and celebration.

 I shout your praises, loving God, for you have forgiven me, and have adopted me as your child and called and empowered me to be your servant. Grant that I may be faithful.

Look for an opportunity to assure someone else of God's forgiveness.

■ OUR TROUBLES AND GOD'S PURPOSES

Psalm 138: "Though I walk in the midst of trouble . . . the Lord will fulfill his purpose for me" (vv. 7-8).

W e can deal with many problems that come our way if we see some purpose behind them. The pain and grief that leave us empty and spent are those that serve no apparent purpose and allow us nothing to hold on to. The result is despair.

The psalmist expressed a sincere hope that even this can be overcome. He was hopeful that despite such agonizing experiences, "the Lord will fulfill his purpose for me." The New Testament revelation of God's love for us through Jesus Christ and his presence within us by way of his Holy Spirit greatly intensifies that hope. There is no logic or meaning in some of the troubles that afflict us. There is, nevertheless, in them or despite them, the hope that the Lord will fulfill his purpose for our lives.

The astonishing thing about the Christian life is that God will often turn the very troubles that could destroy his followers into a means of strengthening and maturing them and enabling them, thereby, to accomplish his purpose. "Give thanks in *all* circumstances," Paul wrote, "for this is God's will for you in Christ Jesus" (1 Thess. 5:18).

 O God, it is only by your miracle-working power that you can fulfill your purpose for me even in and through the troubles that beset me.

Today affirm: "The Lord will fulfill his purpose for me."

■ WHEN WE ARE LONELY

Psalm 139: "You hem me in—behind and before; you have laid your hand upon me" (v. 5).

Perhaps it is loneliness that makes suffering truly critical. We become centered in ourselves and are left to bear something that no human being is meant to bear alone. Friends who know of our pain or troubles may sincerely try to help us, but often, like Job's friends, their advice simply does not meet our needs. While it is God's intention that his concern and love be tangibly expressed through others about us, it doesn't always work out that way.

The psalmist discovered that he was never alone, that there is no place where he could be alone. Like "The Hound of Heaven," God pursued him and stayed close to him.

This is our experience as the beloved children of God. He is behind us, before us, above us, and below us. There is no place or time in which we can be alone. He has been with us in the past and already occupies the places and positions we will occupy in the future. There are times when this glorious truth may be discomfiting, but when we face troubles, it can be comforting and strength-giving. "I praise you because I am fearfully and wonderfully made. Your works are wonderful."

 I am grateful, God, that I can never hide from you, that you can and will always seek me out to restore me to the circle of your love.

Read Francis Thompson's poem, "The Hound of Heaven."

■ SOMEONE DOES CARE FOR US

Psalm 142:   "No one cares for me" (v. 4 TEV).

No one cares for me," agonized the psalmist on one of the blue Mondays of his life. The statement is attributed to David while he was hiding from King Saul in a dark cave.

There are caves along our sojourn through life, and we duck into them now and then to hide from something that threatens us, and there we moan out our loneliness and despair—telling ourselves lies about God's indifference.

It is true that God's love, usually transmitted by way of men and women who have encountered him, is often made ambiguous by human insensitivity. Yet over and above the fallibilities of human beings is the perpetual and eternal truth of God's love and concern for us. "Cast all your anxiety on him," wrote Peter, "because he cares for you" (1 Peter 5:7).

The time has come for us to emerge from our sorry little caves of self-pity and face up to the "King Sauls" that intimidate us. We don't have to be afraid, for God really cares about us.

O God, overwhelm my anxious and troubled heart with your love and peace. Deliver me from distractions and free me from foolish anxieties to live and serve in the center of your divine will.

Memorize 1 Peter 5:7.

■ BURNED BUT NOT CONSUMED

Isa. 43:1-7:   "When you walk through fire, you will not be burned; the flames will not set you ablaze. For I am the Lord, your God" (v. 2).

Life is transmitted through struggle. It is thus that a mother gives birth to a child. It follows in the child's development from the day of breast-weaning to his or her first day at school, from the struggle of learning through the day-by-day, hand-to-mouth existence in a competitive and trouble-fraught world.

God does not promise to deliver us from life's struggles; he did promise to keep us safe and whole amid them. He does not shield us from the pains of our many wounds; he does enable us to bear them. It is by his grace that we live daily in the crucible of conflict. It may even be necessary for God's servants —to purge and prepare them for productive service— and God has no way of tangibly relating to suffering humanity except through his servants who are immersed in humanity's troubles and conflicts.

God may not calm the forces and gales that beat around us, but he can calm the storm that rages in our hearts. He is with us as we pass through the cascading rivers and consuming fires of this life.

You know, O God, my conflicts and many defeats—and you know how incapable I am of fighting my battles alone. Grant me the grace to endure and to show loving concern for others who are in conflict.

Read Daniel 3.

■ WHEN THE TEMPESTS RAGE

Matt. 8:23-27: "You of little faith, why are you so afraid?" (v. 26).

Our Lord and his disciples were crossing the sea in a small boat when a storm suddenly broke, and their vessel was swamped. Jesus was sleeping, but the disciples became panicky and screamed to him to do something. Awakening, Jesus commanded the storm to abate and there was dead calm.

Jesus warned that there will be storms in our lives. We are often like those disciples, panic-stricken, frightened out of our wits, beating the air for something to cling to. Jesus says to us what he said to those disciples: "Why are you such cowards? How little faith you have! I have created, redeemed, and appointed you for just such times as these. I am always with you, indwelling you, empowering you, working out my will through you. Trust me; I won't let you go. There is a quiet harbor somewhere at the end of your journey, but for now you are to abide in me and to work for me in the midst of raging tempests."

It is thus that Christ lovingly rebukes us for allowing the tempests that surround our lives to frighten us and cause doubts about his love and concern for us. He is with us amid the storms that assail us.

 The tempests continue to rage, O Lord, and I am often frightened. I accept you as my Master and Pilot. Help me to trust you, and to show concern for others in the storms they must endure.

Read or sing the hymn "Jesus, Savior, Pilot Me."

■ OUR WORTH IN GOD'S EYES

Matt. 10:24-31:   ". . . you are worth more than many sparrows" (v. 31).

Jesus knows all about the fear and oppression of our world. He was immersed in its darkness, confronted by its enemies, and he suffered its persecutions. He is aware that the forces of evil are seeking mercilessly to disrupt our lives—even to destroy our souls. These evil powers never rest, nor do the trials and tribulations they perpetrate upon us.

But neither does our heavenly Father rest. He is not unaware of the troubles that afflict us. He is ever awake and fully aware of our fears and frustrations. He knows and loves each of us. He who knows when a sparrow falls to the ground, or a young doe is attacked and devoured by a beast of the forest, surely knows us, our trials and troubles, sorrows and sufferings. Although we may not experience any supernatural deliverances from our afflictions, he does through his loving grace reach out to steady and comfort us.

We will be despairing and fearful at times, and doubts will cloud our minds. We will not always feel the nearness of God. We may even wonder, as did Jesus in those terrible moments on the cross, if God has abandoned us. God has not; he is never far off. He will, in his own good time, deliver us from the darkness that confounds us, the troubles that plague us, for we are of great value to our heavenly Father.

 O Lord, so often I feel defeated and diminished by the troubles that assail me. Help me to realize anew my value and importance in your eyes and to find joy in being your disciple.

The next time you see a sparrow, remember that you are of great value to God your Creator.

■ THE CHRISTIAN AND THE CROSS

Mark 8:31-35:   "If anyone would come after me, he must deny himself and take up his cross and follow me" (v. 34).

Christ's call to discipleship invites us to a life of trouble and suffering. It demands self-denial and cross-carrying—the willingness to suffer in our concern and caring for others. "Foxes have holes and birds of the air have nests, but the Son of Man has no place to lay his head" he informed one person who wanted to follow him (Luke 9:58). He required of his disciples a devotion to him and his purposes that would take priority over all other relationships—even to parents and spouses and children.

This kind of devotion and obedience to God spells trouble of one sort or another for all who would be the disciples of Jesus. Abraham was called to get out of his country and his father's house that he might be of use to God. Jeremiah was commanded to deny himself the greatest joys of life, such as wife and children, in order to follow God's plan for his life. It may wring our hearts to oppose the opinions of those we love, but even this is sometimes necessary if we are to follow Christ.

"Whosoever loses his life for me and for the gospel will save it," Jesus promised. May God enable us to pay the price of discipleship—and may he heal the hurts in the lives of others caused by our obedience to our God.

 Dear Lord, you have invited me to share with you the trials and sufferings of your children in this world. Grant, O Lord, that I not fail or disappoint you.

Wear a cross to remind yourself of Christ's call to discipleship.

■ REASON AND THE BIBLE

John 5:39-40:   "These are the Scriptures that testify about me" (v. 39).

During World War II a soldier's life was spared by a New Testament in his breast pocket that prevented a bullet from entering his body. Some enterprising manufacturer subsequently put out little metal-backed New Testaments for soldiers' breast pockets, a sort of charm to ward off enemy bullets. There are Christians who treat the Bible as if it had magical powers to shield them from evil.

The true Word of God is Jesus Christ. The Bible, written by men inspired by God, is the means by which that Word is brought to us. The Bible is essential to our faith; reason enables us to understand that we can't twist its words and promises to apply to deliverance from every trouble or tragedy that besets us.

Rather than deliver us from our troubles, the Bible reveals that loving God who makes us his own and stays with us in the midst of our adversities. Written by men who went through terrible suffering and became martyrs to the faith, the Bible bolsters our courage to face life's tribulations. The biblical authors proclaim the amazing message that God cares about us and will hold on to us despite the evil winds that blow our way.

 Thank you, God, for the written testimonies of your servants as to your saving and sustaining power over those who trust in you.

Make Bible reading a part of each day.

■ IF TROUBLED ABOUT DEATH

John 11:17-27: "He who believes in me will live, even though he dies" (v. 25).

W e cannot entirely obliterate the ugliness of death or erase its horror. As surely as comes the end of summer, so surely must we face up to the fact of death, its parting of the ways, its incomprehensible darkness.

Yet we need not be afraid. "Even though I walk through the valley of the shadow of death, I will fear no evil, for you are with me; your rod and your staff, they comfort me" (Ps. 23:4). We are indeed walking through the valley of the shadow. We never need to pray, as did the psalmist, "Lord, let me know how fleeting is my life" (Ps. 39:4). We know all that we need to know about our end; we know that it is only the beginning of that new and everlasting life that is beyond human description or comprehension.

The resurrection of Jesus Christ is our comfort, because it cancels out the need for foreboding and fear in respect to death. It makes our death an important and even glorious event that completes our creation and unites us totally and consummately with our Creator. Baptism is the door to the church militant; death is the door to the church triumphant. "Whether we live or die, we belong to the Lord" (Rom. 14:8).

 O Lord, help me to believe that you were truly raised from the dead, and help me to demonstrate your resurrection power in my life and my relationships to others.

Memorize Romans 14:8.

48

■ WE ARE HIS FOREVER

John 10:22-30: ". . . and no one can snatch them out of my hand" (v. 28).

"Cast all your anxiety on him because he cares for you," wrote Peter concerning the Christ in one of his letters (1 Peter 5:7). No one says it better than Jesus himself: "My sheep listen to my voice. . . . I give them eternal life, and they shall never perish; no one shall snatch them out of my hand."

Jesus does not coerce us into following him, but if following him is our desire and determination, nothing can stand between us and God's purpose for our lives. No matter how tempestuous the elements about us or how rough the road before us, he is always with us. We are eternally secure in him.

Do we realize what this means? We do not have to grope about in doubt and darkness. We don't have to perpetually question our identity or validity. We never need to feel alone or unloved or lost or insecure —whatever the world's cruel circumstances.

Nothing, no pain or sorrow or defeat or trouble, can alter our status and significance. We belong to God, Jesus is our Savior and our Lord, and no one shall snatch us out of his hand.

 Despite my trials and troubles, O Lord, how comforting it is to know that my relationship to you is secure, that nothing can take me from you. I offer my thanksgiving for your everlasting love.

Find a picture of Jesus as the Good Shepherd. Place it where it will remind you of God's care.

■ OUR ALTERNATIVE TO TROUBLE

John 14:1-7: "Do not let your hearts be troubled. Trust in God; trust also in me" (v. 1).

Paul reflected this injunction of our Lord when he wrote: "Do not be anxious about anything, but in everything, by prayer and petition, with thanksgiving, present your requests to God" (Phil. 4:6). Jesus was preparing his disciples for a time of trial and tribulation. Paul, a post-resurrection disciple, through his own experience with life's troubles and trials passed on this message of hope to the Christians at Philippi. And thus it has passed on to us.

Nevertheless, our hearts will be troubled; our bodies will feel pain. Jesus did not promise peace and contentment as the world interprets it. He did, however, make it indisputably clear that we need not be anxious or troubled about our relationship with him. Instead, he promised to flood our lives with the peace that God grants to those who yield their lives to his saving grace.

In the midst of troubled times and painful circumstances we do not have to allow our hearts to be troubled. We are secure in our relationship to God irrespective of what happens to us or about us. Regardless of the conflicts we encounter or the tempests that batter our lives, he grants us the grace to endure—and ultimately to overcome.

 Teach me, dear God, how to remain serene and anxiety-free even in the midst of the troubled times in which I live.

When you feel troubled, repeat silently (or aloud), "I trust in you, O Lord."

■ BEING GUIDED IN THE TRUTH

John 16:12-15:   "He will guide you into all truth"
(v. 13).

We cannot explain those many occasions when God did not or would not intervene to deliver his children from troubles and calamities. Neither can we deny those numerous instances when prayers for deliverance were answered, people were healed, problems were solved. We celebrate those exhilarating happenings and praise God for those deliverances.

Jesus promised his disciples that he would come through for them. "I will ask the Father, and he will give you another Helper, who will stay with you forever. He is the Spirit, who reveals the truth about God" (John 14:16-17 TEV).

One of the reasons for much of our agony and despair in the trials and tribulations we experience may be due to our lack of conviction about the presence of God's Spirit in our lives. If we accept the concept that God is limited in his activity in our world, we have to realize that his limitations, in some instances, are due to the faltering faith of his children. He has no hands but our hands, and when they hang limp in despair or rigid with fear, they are hardly active in carrying out his purposes and communicating his grace and power to his human creatures about us.

The key to God's invisible presence in our world and in our lives is Pentecost. It happens to every Christian. Jesus has promised, "He will guide you into all truth."

  "Spirit of the living God, fall afresh on me."

Let this be your affirmation today: "The Holy Spirit is guiding me into all truth."

■ THE "LITTLE WHILES" OF PAIN

John 14:15-24: "When I go, you will not be left all alone" (v. 18 TEV).

Jesus cannot shield us from the suffering that permeates our world and touches our individual lives, anymore than he could protect his beloved disciples from the dark hours they were about to enter during his betrayal and execution. Nevertheless, his promise to his disciples is his promise to us: "You will not be left alone."

We exist within the "little while" of Christ's physical absence. This "little while" began when Jesus left his disciples to return to his Father. It will continue until he returns to gather the faithful into his kingdom. Jesus knows that this period will often be a time of sorrow and loneliness and darkness for those who follow him. There will be times when we find ourselves doubting the very existence of a loving God.

The Spirit of Christ was with those first disciples through the terrible sufferings they endured in their service to Christ and their fellow persons—succoring, sustaining, strengthening, holding before them the joy and hope of life everlasting. The Spirit that undergirded and uplifted them, indwelt them and reached out to others through them, is the same Spirit that abides within and about us. Truly, he has not left us alone.

 Spirit of the living God and the resurrected Christ, overcome the desolation and despair of my life and manifest your life and power and peace through me.

Do you know someone who is alone? Reach out to that person with a visit, a call, or a letter.

■ FROM DUST TO DEITY

John 14:23-29:   "Peace I leave with you; my peace I give you" (v. 27).

The Genesis story of creation tells how "God formed man from the dust of the ground, and breathed into his nostrils the breath of life, and man became a living being." In a strange and wonderful way our God is still involved in creating—taking the dust of this world's darkness and oppression, the wrecks that humans make of their lives, and breathing into them his deity. The very heartaches and agonies, the inscrutable difficulties, the insurmountable problems of people's lives are as important in this process of creation and transformation as are the joys, the hours of achievement and accomplishment.

It is thus that he grants us a secure basis for overcoming, or for learning how to live with, the sufferings and conflicts and dark hours that come our way. For one thing, Jesus reveals to us *the love of the Father* (v. 23). There is *the indwelling of the Holy Spirit* (v. 26). And then there is *the peace of Jesus Christ* (v. 27).

What a formula for joyful, effective, secure living—and for meeting the adversities of life with confidence and courage! How can we miss with all this going for us? Despite occasional faltering and floundering, we will grow and mature into healthy Christians and effective ministers of our great and loving God.

 O God, may your eternal love, the indwelling of your Spirit, and your gift of peace crowd out my troubles and accomplish your purposes in my life.

Whenever you feel anxious, repeat Jesus' promise, "Peace I leave with you; my peace I give you."

■ THE TROUBLES OF OUR TIMES

John 16:25-33: "In this world you will have trouble" (v. 33).

Could Jesus have foreseen that God's creatures would be capable of destroying this world and most of its inhabitants in the matter of hours, that over-population, polluted air and water, radioactive wastes, would be threatening to make our planet unfit for human habitation? "In the world you will have trouble," he said, but who could have foreseen this?

Jesus did forecast troubles for us, and challenges us to demonstrate courage and fortitude in dealing with them. He also taught that we are to be the *interveners of God* in the troubles of our times. God intervenes in this world's affairs through his redeemed and empowered servants. We are those servants. Paul wrote that "God chose the foolish things of the world to shame the wise . . . the weak things of the world to shame the strong . . . the lowly things of this world . . . to nullify the things that are" (1 Cor. 1:27-28).

Maybe we would be less threatened by our personal conflicts and consternations if we would involve ourselves in being God's servants and interveners in the problems of our community, nation, and world. We can begin with the people around us to whom we can minister in concern and love. This is the reason we are here.

 Equip me through your Spirit, O God, to bring peace and joy into the pain-ridden lives of people in our broken world.

Identify one problem in your community or the world. Decide what you can do about it and take action.

■ THE ETERNAL HOPE

John 16:16-22: "You will grieve, but your grief will turn to joy" (v. 20).

"Now is your time of grief," Jesus said to his disciples as he approached the final hours of his earthly sojourn, "but I will see you again and you will rejoice." If the disciples had really believed Jesus' words, they may not have been so grief-stricken and frightened through those ugly days of their Lord's trial and crucifixion.

Jesus fulfilled his promise. He did return to them as the resurrected Christ. On several occasions he appeared to them, until they were fully convinced that he was truly the Lord they had followed. Then he left them again in his ascension, only to return through his Spirit on the day of Pentecost. That Spirit, the Spirit of our Christ and God, has been the Christian's comfort and motivation from that day until this.

"Now is your time of grief," our Lord says to us. Even with his indwelling Spirit, we sorrow and suffer in our lives. "But I will see you again and you will rejoice." He is about to make his final appearance, and this will be the end to all our troubles. In the meantime, his Spirit abides within us; the promise of his return is before us. Let us temper our sufferings and crowd out our troubles with rejoicing!

 I do have sorrow now, dear Lord. Establish and strengthen my faith in believing that it will eventually lead to joy—the kind of joy I may share with others who are suffering.

Memorize Jesus' promise in John 16:20.

■ HOW MUCH HE LOVES US!

John 17:6-19:   "I pray for them . . . for those you
have given me, for they are yours" (v. 9).

If there is anything that should comfort us in our
adverse and trouble-ridden world, it is the fact that
Jesus prays for us.

He prays *that we have his joy fulfilled in us*. He is
not referring only to that effervescence and ecstasy
that accompanies the religious experiences of some
people, but to true joy, eternal joy, the joy that filled
the life of Jesus even while he faced betrayal and
execution. This joy abides in us in the midst of the
world's catastrophes.

He prays *that we be kept*. We will often fail; we
will at times become depressed and discouraged in
our defeats and imperfections. In it all and through it
all, Jesus prays that we will be kept.

He prays, not that we should be spared the conflicts
and struggles of this sometimes cruel and
contemptuous world, but *that we might walk in the
truth.*

How much our Lord loves us! May our response to
such love be demonstrated in our love for one
another and our determination to communicate his
love to our fellow creatures.

I thank you for your unfathomable and eternal
love, O Lord. I will trust you to keep me and
guide me in the way of truth.

**What can you do today to communicate God's love
to someone near you?**

■ SMALL FAITH—LARGE DOUBTS

John 20:26-31: "Blessed are those who have not seen and yet have believed" (v. 29).

In Ingmar Bergman's famous but cynical and despair-laden *Winter Night,* one of the characters shares with his pastor his thoughts about Christ's crucifixion. It was his opinion that our Lord's greatest suffering was not the physical pain of the thorns or the nails or the heavy cross. It was the moment of doubt that came even to the human Christ concerning his Father's love for him. He sensed it only for a moment, but it was the moment of his greatest suffering.

There is a "winter night" or a lonely valley for most of us at some time in our lives. The pain is excruciating; we are utterly alone; our hearts are wrenched by doubts. During those dark hours or long days the memories of past blessings or the words of dear friends bring little comfort. We moan into our pillows or stumble about blindly, barely knowing when the sun rises or sets.

Maybe Thomas felt like a "winter night" after Christ's crucifixion. This may have been the reason for Jesus' special revelation to him. Thomas saw, and he believed. Some of us are not that fortunate. We have to do what Jesus did on the cross in his final outcry: "Father, into your hands I commit my spirit." If our prayer is sincere, that is enough. God will hear and respond.

O Lord, I, in my humanness, want so much to see you, touch you, to strongly feel your loving presence. Help me to grow in faith, to be "sure of what I hope for and certain of what I do not see" (Heb. 11:1).

When you are oppressed by doubts, pray, "Father, into your hands I commit my spirit."

■ REJOICING IN SUFFERING?

Rom. 5:1-5: ". . . we also rejoice in our sufferings
. . ." (v. 3).

It is difficult to imagine reaching that state in life
where we can actually "rejoice in our sufferings." Yet
Paul learned the hard way that physical pain or
mental anguish, material loss or overwhelming
sorrow, do not separate us from God nor alter our
relationship to him. We cling to what God has done
for us through Christ, irrespective of our human
feelings and frailties, the very conflicts that threaten
to destroy us become God's tools to grind and polish
and temper our spirits and prepare us for loving and
obedient service to him and our fellow beings.

Perhaps the person who has no trouble or conflict in
life, if such is possible, is the one to be pitied. He or
she would remain a spiritual dwarf unlikely to make
much of a contribution to the welfare of humanity.

Blessed are they who struggle, for they shall become
strong. If we remain sensitive to divine leading,
receptive to divine enablement, and open always to
God's outflowing grace, we shall, in spite of occasional
failures, become stronger through our struggles, even
rejoice in them, and live to claim eternal victory.

Grant me the grace and the courage, O God, to
struggle against the demons that tempt, the
pressures that pull this way and that, and to
mature in my relationship to you and my
responsibilities toward others.

**Can you find any way in which you can rejoice in
your suffering?**

■ FOR THOSE WHO FEEL WRETCHED

Rom. 7:21—8:1:   "Who will rescue me . . . ?" (v. 24).

Sometimes we do feel wretched. We have the desire, even the determination, to do what is right, but we do not in ourselves have the power. The result is failure and frustration, and we are driven to the wall in despair. This makes for conflict that in some measure will persist as long as we live in this world.

While there is little explanation for much that transpires in our lives and our world, this is the one gigantic problem for which God's Word has an answer. It is expressed by Paul who wrote: "There is now no condemnation for those who are in Christ Jesus."

Our failures to measure up must, of course, be acknowledged and confessed. Covert guilt will be destructive to life and personality. Confrontation and confession is not a once-for-all event, but part of our daily relationship to God. When this is followed by surrendering to and embracing the forgiving and renewing grace of God, we can then celebrate like Paul: "Thanks be to God—through Jesus Christ our Lord!"

> I may fail miserably and hurt deeply, but thanks to you, O Lord, I am not wretched. I have been redeemed and reconciled to you forever. Help me turn my feelings of wretchedness into wrestling with the great truths of my redemption through your cross and resurrection.

Whenever failure makes you feel wretched, remind yourself, "There is now *no condemnation* for those who are in Christ Jesus."

■ SUFFERING AS A PREREQUISITE

Rom. 8:12-18: ". . . if indeed we share in his sufferings in order that we may also share in his glory" (v. 17).

While Scripture certainly informs us that sufferings will come to us, we are never enjoined to seek out suffering like those who attempt to find God through self-inflicted pain. Yet Paul sounds as if the prerequisite to being glorified with Christ is to suffer with him.

Paul declares, "We have been justified through faith" (Rom. 5:1) and "by grace we have been saved, through faith—and this . . . is the gift of God" (Eph. 2:8). Where, then, does suffering come in? It is not a prerequisite for an authentic commitment to Christ, but it may be a consequence of it.

Our suffering is not a judgment of God or a punishment for our sinfulness. Some of the troubles we encounter may well be a consequence of our mistakes and wrong-doings, but they do not come from God. The troubles or sufferings we encounter as a consequence of loving and serving God, however, have a redemptive quality, because he can bless and use them for our growth as his children and our productivity as his servants.

The fact that we "share in his sufferings" undergirds our assurance that "we may also share in his glory." And the sufferings we endure, Paul adds, "are not worth comparing with the glory that will be revealed in us."

I accept by your grace, my Lord, whatever suffering I must endure as a consequence of following you. When troubles come my way, enable me to hold firm to my resolve.

Have you ever suffered as a consequence of following Christ?

■ IT'S INCREDIBLE!

Rom. 8:28-30: ". . . in all things God works for the good of those who love him, who have been called according to his purpose" (v. 28).

It's incredible! If it were not for the hundreds of thousands of Christians throughout the centuries who found it to be true, it would be impossible for most of us to take Paul seriously. Is this just some emotional statement that slipped through Paul's pen, or does he really mean it?

He means it! And it throws a whole new light on the troubles and sufferings of God's children. The troubles that confront us, the attacks of Satan, even the consequences of the sins we have committed and confessed, can work for good with "those who have been called according to his purpose." This is not the answer to the problem of pain; it will not obliterate or even reduce the agony of some of our suffering. Yet it does remove its sting and strengthen our hope. It makes us better able to cope—whatever our troubles may be.

We too are "called according to his purpose," so Paul is speaking to us today. Our troubles notwithstanding, let us grab on to Paul's incredible proclamation and rise above our suffering to praise our ever-loving, all-powerful, eternal God!

 Thank you for this splendid revelation, O Lord. I accept it with awe and wonder and rededicate my life to your purposes.

In the midst of your troubles, say, "I believe that God is working for my good in this situation."

■ GOD IS FOR US

Rom. 8:31-35: "If God is for us, who can be against us?" (v. 31).

God is for us; he is on our side. And this is true whatever the problems, conflicts, sufferings or troubles that assail us. This was Paul's experience and is the testimony of countless believers.

"Who shall separate us from the love of Christ? Shall trouble or hardship or persecution or famine or nakedness or danger or sword?" Let us take that question and add on to it our specific trouble or problem, whatever it is that causes us anxiety. Do we dare to believe that our relatively small problems are too big for God, that the God who raised our Lord from the dead cannot stand with us and ultimately raise us out of the troubles that plague us? If so, we are kowtowing to the wrong god, not the God who was revealed through the cross and the resurrection of Jesus Christ.

May the Spirit of the true God break through the numbness of our finite thinking and reveal to us something of who we are and what we have become through Christ. He is Lord over all, and we are his church, his body, the extension of Christ in this world. He is for us, on our side— forever. How immeasurably and infinitely blessed we are!

 O God, is it possible that the troubles that besiege me indicate that I am on course in my relationship to you, that you are truly on my side? If so, I am blessed indeed.

Say to yourself today: "God is for me. God is on my side."

■ WE ARE THE WINNERS

Rom. 8:37-39: ". . . we are more than conquerors through him who loved us" (v. 37).

Regardless of the troubles that assail us, the sufferings that lay us low, the conflicts that beat us down or burn us out, we are the ultimate winners—"more than conquerors through him who loved us." This is because there is nothing that can come between us and our loving God. Nothing, that is, unless we neglect to hear and abide by God's Word or fail to rely on his grace.

The tragedies and conflicts of this life will discourage us, but they can in no way change God's attitude or nullify his promises or stifle his love for us. Failures and defeats may trip us up, but they do not affect our relationship to God. Our boat will rock; the earth will tremble; revolutions will shake up governments and institutions. Our traditions may be endangered, our convictions threatened, every temporal security collapsed, but God's love and reconciling grace are forever, and he will never let us go.

Nothing, absolutely nothing can separate us from the love of God as revealed, proclaimed, and demonstrated through Jesus Christ. We are the sons and daughters of God, his servants and disciples forever.

 My heart is filled with praises, my God, because your Spirit active in the resurrection of Christ is now active in my life. Whatever the trials and troubles that stand in my way, nothing can separate me from your eternal love, and I will by your grace be a conqueror.

Memorize Romans 8:37.

■ LIVING WITH OUR TROUBLES

Rom. 12:9-13: "Be joyful in hope, patient in affliction, faithful in prayer" (v. 12).

Hope, affliction, prayer—they all go together in the Christian life. It was certainly true in Paul's day, and he exhorts his fellow believers to live as Christians ought to live from day to day.

While some of us have gone through periods that were relatively free of serious troubles or problems, we live in a world crowded with suffering people. Plagues, droughts, catastrophes, and calamities are happening in many places around our globe, leaving hundreds of thousands of dying, suffering people in their wake. Some of these things may happen to us.

Paul's recipe for living with trouble is as relevant for us as it was for the first-century Christians. Rejoicing in that hope that grants us life may be the only thing that will sustain us in our nuclear world. Suffering patiently the pains and trials that come our way is expected of all God's servants. Keeping in tune with God and his purposes will result in strength and courage as we draw on his grace to love and serve in the midst of suffering.

 O God of love, through the cross and the empty tomb of Christ you have granted me a hope that will never die. With this eternal hope I can meet my trials with prayer and patience and can even rejoice in your redeeming love.

Choose a prayer from those at the end of this book.

■ LET'S BE REASONABLE

1 Cor. 13:9-13: "When I became a man, I put childish ways behind me" (v. 11).

Someone has said, "The task of reason is to make impossible all religions save the best." While the content of Christianity will not be contained by reason neither can it leave the mind behind. The Christian faith is most certainly reasonable, and the New Testament writers declare that God does not will the troubles or pain or sorrow we are facing. They are caused by our own doing, or the actions of others, or the random forces of nature. The faith of those Christians who regard everything that happens to them, be it joyful or painful, as sent and controlled by God is a childish faith—a faith that has never grown or matured. Paul encourages us to "stop thinking like children . . . in your thinking be adults" (1 Cor. 14:20).

God does not *will* the starving millions or the threatening nuclear Armageddon or the fires and earthquakes and floods. "The powers of this dark world . . . the spiritual forces of evil" may will it, but not God. Until we mature in our faith to this level of understanding, we may never be able to cope with the problems confronting us.

God does allow us to go through the fire and endure the crucible, but God promises that the ultimate victory will be ours.

 Some troubles are inescapable, and many problems unsolvable, but I thank you, O Lord, for the answers I need as your child and servant.

Is there any childish thinking that you need to leave behind?

■ WHEN YOU DESPAIR OF LIFE ITSELF

2 Cor. 1:3-11: "We were under great pressure, far beyond our ability to endure, so that we despaired even of life" (v. 8).

It probably isn't true that everyone has suicidal thoughts at some time in life; such thoughts, however, are certainly not unusual. We know of those who have had such experiences; it may happen to us—that we are so crushed by some terrible loss or suffering that "we despaired even of life."

Many who have recovered from some such crushing experiences bear witness to the power of faith in the resurrected Christ. While God may not shield his children from this kind of suffering, his miracle-working power is indeed manifest in remarkable deliverances from such experiences. As the crucified Christ was raised from the dead by the power of God's Spirit, so his followers are raised from their crushing despair.

It is seldom an instantaneous recovery. It is usually slow and painful. Paul credits such experiences with teaching him the need of relying on the power of God. This is something we must learn if we are to discover how to be his joyful, faithful, and effective servants. And this we will do by the grace of God.

"For just as the sufferings of Christ flow over into our lives, so also through Christ our comfort overflows."

O God, break through the blackness of my despair with the shining light of victory—that victory won for me by way of the cross and the empty tomb. Only then can I overcome despair and celebrate life.

Has there been a time when you have despaired of life? How did God deliver you?

■ POSITIVE REFLECTIONS ON NEGATIVE EXPERIENCES

2 Cor. 4:7-12: "We are often troubled, but not crushed" (v. 8 TEV).

The apostle Paul is only one of a countless number of believers who have demonstrated that troubles and tribulations are not the end of life but often a new beginning to fruitful living. While God does not initiate the miseries that beset his children, he is lovingly and powerfully able to turn them into pruning hooks that make for enrichment and fruition.

Paul declared, "We have this treasure . . . so we do not lose heart." Nor should any of us. The pain and sorrow may not be any less, but the hope is there and the final victory is assured. Troubled, afflicted, confounded, persecuted, beaten down, but we will not be wiped out. "Everything he has is in your power," said God to Satan, "but you must not hurt Job himself" (Job 1:12 TEV). The power Satan has in our world, or the random ravages of nature's forces, may not be forestalled by our omnipotent Creator and Redeemer; but if our patience is long and our courage strong, we will discover new blessings as a consequence of our sufferings.

God created us in his image. He will not allow that image to be destroyed—whatever the trials and conflicts that assail us.

 Sometimes, O Lord, I feel both troubled and crushed. While you do not eliminate the troubles that come my way, I find hope in your promise that you will not allow them to sever my relationship with you.

Recall a time when God brought you through trouble. Try to share the memory with someone else.

■ ENDURING FOR JESUS' SAKE

2 Cor. 6:3-10:   ". . . as servants of God we
commend ourselves . . . in great endurance; in
troubles, hardships and distresses . . ." (v. 4).

As the Father has sent me, I am sending you," Jesus
said to his disciples (John 20:21). He also said, "I am
sending you out like lambs among wolves" (Luke
10:3). He certainly wasn't promising a quiet country
lane or a lily-strewn path for those who follow him.
In contrast to modern preachers who concentrate on
the perpetual joy and ecstatic feelings that are
supposed to flood the lives of those who come to
Christ, our Lord and the disciples who followed him
discovered a great deal of "troubles, hardships and
distresses" in their efforts to serve God.

The troubles we encounter may be the kind that we
are called upon to endure rather than something from
which we must be delivered. While they do not come
from God, they are as much a part of this world as
birth and death, hunger and thirst. In order to become
lovingly involved in the sufferings of others, we must
expect discomfort and pain, even illness and possible
death. This was certainly the lot of those first disciples,
most of whom experienced imprisonment and
martyrdom in the course of their ministry.

Saints before us suffered many things in order that
the good news might come to us. Should we expect
less as we minister within our broken and pain-ridden
world?

 O Lord, may my dedication to you and your
objectives be so profound that I will anticipate
and be willing to endure suffering for your sake.

**Think of a new way in which you can share God's
love with others.**

■ NO USELESS SUFFERING

1 Cor. 15:12-20: "But Christ has indeed been
raised from the dead . . ." (v. 20).

The relatives of victims who were arrested by the
military of several Latin American countries and
never seen again gathered for a spiritual retreat in
Costa Rica. United in their common sorrow, they
assembled to strengthen and encourage one another.
After several days of being together, a phrase that
these men and women used over and over again to
describe their feelings became a motto: "There is no
useless suffering."

This group of people had every reason for despair
and anger at their sudden and tragic loss of loved
ones. Yet the suffering they felt so keenly they knew
was not suffering in vain. And in this suffering they
knew the meaning of our Lord's resurrection far
better than do most of us. They had become
convinced that the resurrection of Jesus Christ was not
an abstract teaching or theological dogma, but a fact,
making possible a living hope that penetrated to the
depths of their souls. They had profoundly
experienced the sufferings of Christ; they now richly
knew and experienced his resurrected life.

The resurrected Christ puts hope into our suffering,
and even makes it serve his purposes in our lives.
"Thanks be to God! . . . Keep busy always in your
work for the Lord . . . nothing you do in the Lord's
service is ever useless" (1 Cor. 15:57-58 TEV).

 I cannot comprehend it, Lord, but I offer my
praises to you because even my sufferings need
not be useless and without purpose in my life.

Let this be your motto: "There is no useless suffering."

■ CONFRONTING THE INEVITABLE

1 Cor. 15:50-58: "Death has been swallowed up in victory" (v. 54).

My life is a mystery, but death is a dark malady which faith cannot evade. Yet faith has a word; it speaks of process and purpose of which death is a part, and it speaks of something steady over all the wreckage."

"What does it matter who wrote it?" said Carlyle Marney in *Faith in Conflict*. "The agony of every man is in it."

The Christian faith faces death, bluntly and biologically. We are all "walking through the valley of the shadow of death." It is abhorrent to us. It is darker and deeper than any sleep. It is without mercy. It cannot be bought off or evaded. Secular humanists may come to terms with it; religions are concocted that turn it into an illusion or reduce its horror with vague promises of reincarnation. But it remains the final and ultimate evil.

We need not, however, allow it to frighten or trouble us. For the Christian, it is "swallowed up in victory." It is an event on the course to become what God intends each of us to be. For our death becomes, through Jesus Christ, the grand entry into total, eternal completeness. "Do not let your hearts be troubled. . . . I am going there to prepare a place for you" (John 14:1-2).

I thank you, O God of light and life, because you have solved the problem of death with your gift of everlasting life.

Meditate on the truth that Jesus has gone ahead to prepare a place for you.

■ TIME TO BAIL OUT?

2 Cor. 12:1-6:   "I will go on to visions and revelations from the Lord" (v. 1).

Paul's memory of an amazing experience in the beginning of his life as a Christian did much to temper his spirit and give him hope and courage when things became difficult for him. We cannot live on memories alone, but it is well to keep a drawer full of them to pull out and rejoice over when we run up against hard times.

While our memories may not be as stimulating and fulfilling as Paul's, there are the good times when God seemed very real to us. They are those times when we were excited, motivated, and deeply convinced of God's love and presence. We may attribute these to youthful enthusiasm or runaway emotionalism, but we need to realize that God has not changed over the years. He is as loving and as near to us now as he was then.

We cannot revert to the past and recover those feelings of our youth, but we can embrace anew our unchangeable and ever-loving God and charge on— more sedate, perhaps, but wiser, stronger, and more convinced than ever of his power and presence in our lives. This is not the time to "bail out." It is the time for a firmer commitment to God and his purposes and a renewed assurance that God will not sell us short.

 O God, there are times when I just want to stop struggling and go home. But there is no home for me save that to which you have called me. Grant me the grace and determination to keep struggling until I reach the end of my course.

Take time to remember a time when God was especially real to you. Look for an opportunity to share that memory.

■ POWER THROUGH WEAKNESS

2 Cor. 12:7-10:   "My grace is sufficient for you, for my power is made perfect in weakness" (v. 9).

We are not certain what Paul's "thorn in the flesh" was, but it doesn't make much difference. The point is: he faced troubles in his life, and he credited Satan, not God, for this particular affliction. It was the miracle-working God, however, who took a troublesome thing and turned it into a vehicle of usefulness in Paul's ministry.

The Christian faith offers such meaning and power to all of us. It asserts that while God is not the perpetrator of our sufferings, he involves himself in them. He has done this through Christ, who suffered on our behalf and is able to "sympathize with our weaknesses" (Heb. 4:15). He who turned the defeat of the cross into the victory of the empty tomb has made available his power to work similar miracles in our lives.

"My power is made perfect in weakness," wrote Paul. We may not always experience Paul's measure of contentment, but our "thorn in the flesh" may be useful in keeping us close to God and humbly dependent on him for our daily grace. Maybe it will be used by God to enable us to sympathize with others and bring to them the comfort of his eternal love.

 I may never, O Lord, delight in my weaknesses, but I reach out for your grace that will permeate my weaknesses and transform them into channels of your power.

Affirm today: "God's power is made perfect in my weakness."

■ THE SOURCE OF MOST TROUBLES

Eph. 6:10-18:   "Put on the full armor of God so that you can take your stand against the devil's schemes" (v. 11).

There is a world full of evil," wrote Carlyle Marney, "and I am involved. Faith cannot answer evil by watering down the fires of human nature. But the personal encounter of faith releases a transforming power." Paul refers to "the spirit of evil who is now at work in those who are disobedient" (Eph. 2:2). That same spirit is working on the lives of those who are committed to the transforming power of God. And, according to Paul, it is the personal encounter of faith in God's transforming power that is the only defense we have: "take up the shield of faith, with which you can extinguish all the flaming arrows of the evil one."

It is sometimes within the darkness of the troubles and pain that pursue and afflict us that we really begin to see and feel God as he is. There will be times when the only prayer we can utter are those last words of Jesus on that cruel cross: "Father, into your hands I commit my spirit." And that is where we must ultimately and trustingly commit these demon troubles that seek to possess us.

It may be very dark at this moment, but because of Jesus Christ who overcame the evil one by way of the cross and the resurrection, the dawn is not far off.

 Merciful God, I feel impeded, almost suffocated by the dark powers about me. Grab on to me and hold on, Lord, for it's only by your grace that I can survive.

Memorize today's prayer so you can use it throughout the day.

■ SUFFERING WITH CONFIDENCE

Eph. 3:13-21: "I beg you, then, not to be
discouraged because I am suffering for you"
(v. 13 TEV).

Paul's letter to the church at Ephesus is a remarkable
demonstration of how he handled suffering in his
life. He recognized how his suffering was integrally
related to his ministry to his fellow beings. "It is all for
your benefit," he said, and he broke into a song of
thanksgiving and praise that makes up one of the
most exciting and beautiful portions of Scripture.

This kind of suffering was probably not brought on
by his personal distortions and shortcomings, but a
direct result of his attempts to serve God. His
obedience to God and his love for his sisters and
brothers in Christ meant he had to pay the price, to
share Christ's sufferings on their behalf. He did this
joyfully and thankfully.

Not all of our sufferings serve God, but it is possible
that—unknown to us—some of them do, that God can
turn them into blessings for us and for others in the
human family. Whatever the cause of our sufferings,
we do well to turn them over to God with the
confidence that "he is able to do so much more than
we can ever ask for, or even think of . . ." (v. 20 TEV).
This may not reduce the pain, but his power at work
within us will enable us to endure and even to find
peace and joy in the midst of our sufferings.

 I do not pray for deliverance, dear Lord, but I
pray that my suffering may somehow be of use
to you in my relationship to those around me.

**Remind yourself several times today: "God is able to
do much more than I can ever ask for, or even
think of."**

■ SUCCESS THROUGH STRUGGLE

Phil. 1:12-14: ". . . what has happened to me has really served to advance the gospel" (v. 12).

It is amazing—and encouraging—the way in which God is able to turn the unhappy and troublesome things that happen to us, even our foolish errors and failures, into stepping-stones toward the accomplishment of his purposes in our world.

Paul himself was a positive thinker in this respect. Instead of whining in despair over his imprisonment, he wrote beautiful, inspiring letters to churches he had formerly served, informing them that his troubles, which would be regarded as foul-ups by the world, "really served to advance the gospel." The miracle-working power of God is not revealed primarily in remarkable deliverances but in turning unfortunate events, troubles, circumstances, into a means by which his kingdom is advanced throughout the world.

Sometimes our struggles and even our failures lead to success, our defeats to eventual victory, our pains and sorrows to healing and happiness—if not for us, perhaps for others around us. The least we can do, and it may be the only thing we can do, is to commit them all, with our lives and means, into the hands of our loving God and let him take care of the consequences.

 It has happened so often with others, O Lord, that I almost believe it—that these trials and conflicts that come my way may somehow serve your purposes. May it happen through me, dear Lord.

Can you identify any ways in which God has used your troubles to advance his kingdom?

■ SERVING GOD THROUGH SUFFERING

Phil. 1:29–2-13:   "For it has been granted to you on behalf of Christ not only to believe on him, but also to suffer for him" (v. 29).

God provides the grace, but our works measure whether this grace has penetrated us or not," writes W. A. Poovey. The suffering we experience or the trials we live through in no way contribute to our salvation—and this regardless of the sacrifices we make in the name of Christ or for the sake of others. "For it is by grace that you have been saved through faith. It is not the result of your efforts, but God's gift," wrote Paul (Eph. 2:8 TEV). Our willingness to suffer may, however, be a measure of how much God's grace has penetrated and is allowed to work in our lives. Our response to God's gift of grace is a willingness to risk suffering if it comes as a consequence of our serving him or his people.

"We are God's workmanship, created in Christ Jesus to do good works," wrote Paul (Eph. 2:10). There are times when our willingness to suffer, or our joyful encounter with the tribulations that come upon us, is a good work—that we can actually serve God through suffering.

Even this "willingness" or "joyful encounter" with the pains and problems that assault us is possible only by the grace of God. May God grant us this grace.

 I know not, O Lord, whether my suffering is of benefit to anyone else, or if it in some way serves you. But I pray for the wisdom and grace to deal with it.

Affirmation: "I am God's workmanship, created in Christ Jesus to do good works."

76

■ SOMETHING TO THINK ABOUT

Phil. 4:4-7:   "Do not be anxious about anything" (v. 6).

P aul sets an ideal before us: "Do not be anxious about anything." In this life we may never reach this goal, but it is certainly something to aim for in respect to Christian maturity.

The fact is, we are anxious about a great many things. In spite of Christ's injunction not to allow our hearts to be troubled (John 14:1), our hearts are often troubled about one thing or another. This includes the conditions of our world, our economy, the threat of nuclear war, pollution, our jobs and security, our health, our children and their futures.

Maybe Paul did learn to shuck off his anxieties. If so, it was because of his unshakable, unwavering conviction that "the Lord is near." If we really believe that the Christ who died on the cross for our sins was raised from the dead and that the same Spirit active at Christ's resurrection and on the Day of Pentecost indwells our lives, we, too, can become anxiety-free and joy-filled in our daily lives.

 O Lord, how I envy those whose faith is so strong that they are seldom anxious about anything! I don't see how this can happen to me, but I pray that by your grace I may at least shed those needless worries that obstruct your purposes in my life.

What are your major anxieties and worries? Make a special point today of releasing them into God's care.

■ LESSONS TO LEARN

Phil. 4:10-13: ". . . I have learned to be content whatever the circumstances" (v. 11).

The apostle John said that "whoever says that he remains in union with God should live as Jesus Christ did" (1 John 2:6 TEV). How can we emulate *Jesus* when we haven't even been able to measure up to *Paul's* standards? Few of us have learned to be content "whatever the circumstances." We are still acting like spoiled children—pouting, griping, criticizing, stepping on one another, insisting on our way, or scrambling for some position that will boost our ego. We are not always happy with where we are and what we are doing.

This may have something to do with the troubles we fall into. If we are aware that we are not living within God's will for our lives, the first step to dealing with our troubles is to commit ourselves to faith in and obedience to God as revealed through his Word and his Son, our Lord. If we persist in our faith and obedience, we may learn with Paul that whether we are rich or poor, in the valley or on the mount, whether there be sorrow or pain, conflict or defeat, this will not threaten our relationship to God. We may even learn how to find some contentment within our difficult circumstances.

We are God's forever, and we can celebrate forever our adoption and our identity as God's children. He provides us with the strength and courage we need to confront and overcome anything that comes our way.

Loving God, while I may not reach the state of perfect contentment in this life, may I be content with the kind of restlessness that goads me in your direction for my life.

What are the growing edges in your Christian life?

■ REJOICING IN SUFFERING?

Col. 1:24-29: "Now I rejoice in what was suffered for you" (v. 24).

P aul discovered that discipleship meant involvement. Jesus had set the pace and expected his disciples to follow through. Thus Paul identified himself with the agonies of humankind and became involved in its crying needs.

A disciple of Jesus not only accepts Jesus as Savior, but as Lord and Master. To follow Christ means to "complete what still remains of Christ's sufferings" (Col. 1:24 TEV). To do this one must not only criticize the distortions of humanity, but become involved in the blood and tears, the sorrows and sufferings of God's creatures. As Jesus suffered on our behalf, so Christians are expected to suffer on behalf of others, even to losing their lives in service only to truly find them anew in the incomparable joy of being servants of the living and eternal God.

This is a high goal for the Christian, and only the truly committed will ever begin to approach it. It seems to indicate that our sufferings are not always something to be delivered from, but something to be endured and used in our service for Christ among God's children. It is only by God's grace that we, with Paul, can rejoice in our sufferings.

 O Lord, I am still a long way from that point where I can "rejoice in my sufferings." Teach me how to find a measure of joy and contentment and achievement even in the midst of these troubles about me.

What human need or problem concerns you most? How could you become involved in alleviating this situation?

■ WHEN WE HAVE FAILED

1 Tim. 1:12-27: "Christ Jesus came into the world to save sinners—of whom I am the worst. But for that very reason I was shown mercy . . ." (vv. 15-16).

If Paul felt himself to be the worst of sinners, where does that leave us? We are made of such frail stuff. God's promises of peace and joy seem obscure, unreachable. Our sins accelerate; our faith shrivels. We simply are not made of the same materials as were the old saints. These are the thoughts that peck at us like famished buzzards after we have been smashed against the wall by some spirit-suffocating, death-threatening failure—whether that failure be a shameful immorality, a broken marriage, a fouled-up vocation, the harm we have caused a beloved friend, or whatever.

"Here is a trustworthy saying that deserves full acceptance: Christ Jesus came into the world to save sinners." And this includes failures. Our great God has shown us how to start over again. One of life's most precious gifts is the opportunity and the privilege of beginning anew. It is the gift of the ever-loving Creator, revealed through his Son, Jesus Christ. This is for all who have failed. It is to be received and appropriated by faith.

Our failures do not damn or destroy us. They drive us back to God—for forgiveness, acceptance, and the opportunity to rise up and plunge once more into life's battles.

If you, O God, can turn my frail stuff into staunch material that can bless and benefit the lives of others, then, truly, you are a great God.

Affirm today: "Christ Jesus came into the world to save *me*."

■ SUFFERINGS THAT SERVE A PURPOSE

2 Tim. 1:8-12: "Join with me in suffering for the gospel" (v. 8).

We live in an ongoing crisis, the crisis of change in a churning, conflict-ridden world. It is frightening at times, and we may wish to retreat to the sanctuary of the past, where we imagine we could be free from the tensions of this life. We look to the church where we hear those great words of security and safety in a cozy relationship with our God. Yet it does not always prepare us for the Monday-through-Saturday encounters with life and its relationships. We painfully discover risks, dangers, strife, and struggles that seem irreconcilable with the Christian life as we were taught it in childhood.

Our Lord has placed us in the midst of crises. They are all about us. They will cause or be accompanied by pain, sometimes utter despair. Yet this is where we are called, commissioned, and equipped to serve—to bring light into this world's darkness, and hope within this planet's despair, healing to its wounds. God has set us free and granted us his Spirit to enable us to do this. It means, however, that we "endure hardship . . . like a good soldier of Christ Jesus" (2 Tim. 2:3).

Our sufferings, as painful and unpleasant as they are, can serve God's purposes in our world. We never seek them out, but we must accept them as they come, confident that he is able to guard what we have entrusted to him for that day.

 Help me, O God, to accept willingly my share of hardship and trouble for your sake.

Choose a prayer from those at the end of this book.

■ KEEPING THE FAITH

2 Tim. 4:6-8:   "I have fought the good fight . . . I
have kept the faith" (v. 7).

Faith and endurance are closely related. In order to
keep the faith, we must endure; in order to endure,
we must keep the faith. "By faith Abraham . . . Moses
. . . Gideon, Samson, David, Samuel and the
prophets" did all the remarkable, unbelievable things
that made up the history of the Israelites (Heb. 11).
"So do not throw away your confidence. . . . You need
to persevere so that when you have done the will of
God, you will receive what he has promised" (Heb.
10:35-36).

If we are to fight the good fight—and that takes
endurance and courage, a determination to face
head-on the troubles and trials before us—we must
persevere in our faith. It must, however, be the right
faith—faith in God as he is revealed through Jesus
Christ. Trust and confidence in some healer or
counselor may bring immediate or imagined relief for
some pains or problems, but only the true faith will
survive the temptations and tribulations that
threaten us. While it may not make our troubles
disappear, the true faith will give us the courage and
strength to deal with them.

Keeping the faith requires a "good fight." There will
be defeats as well as victories, but the final triumph
is not in question. That has already been established
by the cross and the resurrection of Christ.

> Help me, dear Lord, to understand that faith is
> not simply a leisurely abiding in what you have
> done for me. It is also a striving and struggling
> to lay hold of and use the gifts you daily offer
> to your children.

In what ways are you fighting the good fight?

■ HOLDING FAST

Heb. 4:14-16:   "Let us hold firmly to the faith we profess" (v. 14).

There is good reason for holding firmly, for keeping the faith, because in Jesus Christ "we do not have a high priest who is unable to sympathize with our weaknesses, but we have one who has been tempted in every way, just as we are." It is obvious that we need to renew our faith from time to time, to make sure we keep the faith, lest we back out on our relationship to God and retreat once more into that fruitless struggle to exist apart from God.

We have in Christ not only a Savior, but a Keeper and Guardian over our souls. He is the one who knows our failings and hang-ups, who understands the trials and conflicts that come our way, and who will grant us the grace to come through them unscathed.

There will be wounds, and scars to remind us of those wounds; nevertheless, victory is assured if we stay close to that one who is the giver of divine grace.

"Let us have confidence, then, and approach God's throne, where there is grace. There we will receive mercy and find grace to help us just when we need it" (v. 16 TEV).

> Gracious God, I need your help just to hold on to the faith amidst the troubles that clutter up my course through life. You know the difficulties and problems that harass your children, and you have invited us to request your help. It is thus that I come to you. Give me the courage and strength to receive your mercy and grace.

Meditate on the truth that Jesus has been tempted as we are, so he is able to sympathize with our weakness.

■ SANCTIFICATION THROUGH SUFFERING

Heb. 5:7-9: "Although he was a Son, he learned obedience from what he suffered" (v. 8).

It is still difficult for us to reckon with the humanity of Christ. We are inclined to concoct our own image of him and to regard him as perpetually happy, healthy, all-wise, and all-powerful—as one who didn't have to contend with all the headaches and heartaches that are our lot in life. We are wrong. Although God's Son, in his sinless nature, may not have been tripped up by the petty things that trouble us, he was subject to sufferings and sorrows that were far greater than anything we have to endure. We are not aware of any illnesses that afflicted him. He was not hindered by guilt and its consequences. But he must have been depressed at times. He was hated by the religious leaders, betrayed by some of his followers, nailed to a cross by his enemies, and even, it seemed to him, abandoned by his Father in heaven.

Yet the human Christ, the only begotten Son of God, "learned obedience through what he suffered." While this is far more than we can comprehend, it suggests that the troubles and sufferings that fall upon us may contribute to spiritual life and growth.

It can happen—if we accept them and discover in our faith a God who loves us and enables us to bear them and who, through the suffering Christ, knows, understands, and holds on to us in our sufferings.

 I cannot understand, O God, why the road through life is so rough, why this walk with you is so difficult. Help me to see how my trouble-filled hours do contribute to my spiritual growth and enhance my relationship with you.

Recall times in the life of Jesus when he suffered.

■ OUR FAITH—GOD'S GIFT

Heb. 12:1-2: ". . . let us run with determination the race that lies before us" (v. 1 TEV).

He did not give up because of the cross!" said this writer concerning Christ. "On the contrary, because of the joy that was waiting for him, he thought nothing of the disgrace of dying on the cross . . ." (v. 2 TEV).

To "run with determination" demands faith. Faith is in itself a gift of God. There is, of course, an element of risk and a measure of pain involved in the exercise of this gift. One of the reasons we dare to step out in the face of risk and pain is the faith of those who have gone before us. It was their experience, and it will be ours, that faith does not shield us from the events that wound us. Nevertheless, we discover in these witnesses from history the faith that is capable of embracing suffering and despair and using them as instruments that mature us, make us more sensitive to the hurts of others, and teach us to accept the hardships of our lives. Rather than floundering in every turbulence that engulfs us, we learn how to stand firm against the storm and walk steadily among the vicissitudes of daily life.

"Therefore, strengthen your feeble arms and weak knees. Make level paths for your feet," (Heb. 12:12-13). And run with determination.

Dear Lord, I enthusiastically set out determined to follow and serve you. But my faith falters, my knees buckle, my heart is faint, and I am discouraged and afraid. I believe, O Lord. Help me in my unbelief.

Affirmation: "I will run with determination the race set before me."

■ CONSIDERING OURSELVES FORTUNATE

James 1:2-8: "Consider it pure joy . . . whenever you face trials of many kinds" (v. 1).

W e wonder about those pious people who, when they hit their thumb with a hammer or have a flat tire on their car or drop a stack of dishes, scream out a hallelujah. Perhaps they are farther along in their Christian growth than we are, but the "praise-the-Lord" cries of people in the middle of trouble may be more pretense than piety.

On the other hand, there are sincere Christians who, like Paul, have truly found that there is joy within the trials that they faithfully endure.

We do have much to learn as the children of God. The most difficult, perhaps, is to learn how to regard our trials and tribulations—even the tragedies that beset us—as capable of enhancing and enriching our lives. While we hardly "praise the Lord" *for* these things, we can praise him because he can and does use them to draw us closer to him and thereby accomplish his purposes in and through us.

If we work at it, we may be able to reach that level, by the grace of God, where we can "consider it pure joy" when trouble comes our way.

 I praise you, Lord, for bringing me through past tribulations, but I find no joy in the present trials that assail me. Grant me the faith that will enable me to find some peace and joy in the troubles I face today.

Ask God to use your troubles to draw you closer to him.

■ SOURCE OF MANY TROUBLES

James 4:1-10: "What causes fights and quarrels among you? Don't they come from your desires that battle within you?" (v. 1).

There is a war being waged *within* us, which, if not handled with the grace that God grants, is capable of creating a war *around* us. It is often initiated by the inner urge for self-gratification and self-aggrandizement. There is something on the inside that rebels against the God who created and claims us for himself. At times we yield to these self-serving desires and thereby crowd the Spirit of God into some small corner of our lives, where his influence and control over us and through us is limited. This inner urge for self-gratification, present in all of humanity, is the source of many of our troubles. It is capable of turning us into the enemies of God.

While we cannot, in this life, totally escape the siren calls of humanness, we can resist these urges and instincts, and resist them successfully, if we do so with the grace that God grants to his children.

God's grace becomes active in the lives of those who submit to his love and who give him permission to remold them into vessels for his holy use. This is the only effective way to deal with those troubles whose source is within us. Let us be persistent in our commitment to God's control of our lives and destinies.

 I surrender my passions and desires to you, O God. Weed out the unworthy ones and take control of every fiber of my being.

Are there some inner struggles or desires that you need to yield to the Lord?

■ GIVING THE DEVIL HIS DUE

James 4:7-10: "Resist the devil and he will flee from you" (v. 7).

When hen told that the British were devils, Gandhi retorted by saying: "The only devils in the world are those running in our hearts, and that is where our battles ought to be fought."

Gandhi may not be theologically accurate, but he may have perceptively targeted the cause of many of the abhorrent things that come out of us or happen to us in the course of our lives.

The problem is there is little we can do about the "devils" in our hearts except by the grace of God. Our frequent resolutions and our determined resolve may have little effect on these internal demons. They continue battering our lives, finding loopholes in our self-righteous intentions, firing up our frustrations and fears to make our lives miserable and our objectives unreachable.

Yet we are enjoined to "resist the devil," to make his antics of little consequence and no account. Paul tells us how: "Build up your strength in union with the Lord and by means of his mighty power. Put on all the armor that God gives you, so that you will be able to stand up against the Devil's evil tricks" (Eph. 6:10-11 TEV).

 As you, my Lord, have met the Enemy and canceled out his intentions, so by your gift of strength and grace I will continue to do battle with the forces of evil within me and around me.

What are the "devils" in your heart which you need to resist with God's power?

■ THE LIVING HOPE

1 Peter 1:3-9: ". . . for a little while you may have had to suffer grief in all kinds of trials" (v. 6).

Let us give thanks to the God and Father of our Lord Jesus Christ! Because of his great mercy he gave us new life by raising Jesus Christ from death. This fills us with a living hope. . . . Be glad about this, even though it may now be necessary for you to be sad for a while because of the many kinds of trials you suffer" (vv. 3, 6 TEV).

The troubles will not go away. More often than not, the only way to deal with them is to change our focus. This is possible when we cease commiserating over our adversities and begin concentrating our thoughts on the "living hope" to which we have been born anew through the resurrection of Jesus Christ from the dead.

Peter is suggesting that these various trials we may have to suffer serve to test our faith by showing whether we can be thankful in the midst of trying circumstances. Have not the tragedies that we have experienced contributed in some way to our lives and made us more lovingly sensitive to the sorrows and pains of others? If so, this indicates that our faith is indeed genuine, and that this is the approach we must take in respect to our present and future troubles.

Our faith, however, must be focused on the "living hope." The greatness and beauty of that hope makes even our sufferings seem worthwhile.

There are times, O God, when the living hope is but a pin-prick of light in the darkness of the night. May it burn brightly, Lord, lest I lose my way and become lost to you and your purposes.

Today focus on the "living hope" you have in Jesus.

■ CALLED TO SUFFER

1 Peter 2:13-21: "Christ suffered for you, leaving you an example, that you should follow in his steps" (v. 21).

To this you were called," wrote Peter, stating that suffering for that which is right has God's approval and that the supreme model for this kind of suffering is Jesus Christ himself. This assurance does little to remove the pain and frustration of our daily encounters with life's troubles, but puts point and purpose into those conflicts that come about in the advancement of God's objectives.

We can never measure up to the example that Christ has left for us to follow. Few of us will meet the high standard of sacrificial love that Peter and Paul attained in their ministry. We cannot even make a beginning in that course save by God's grace. God *has* showered upon us his grace, and to this high standard we were called. It is up to us to make a move in this direction, to receive his grace, and to commit ourselves to his loving will for our lives, no matter what troubles may ensue as a consequence of that commitment.

We are not to seek out suffering; it will eventually seek us out. We might well expect it. God will enable us to endure it; and we may rejoice in his approval when it comes.

I know you suffered for me, Jesus. I praise and glorify you. I am not so willing to contemplate suffering on your behalf. The grace and strength and courage must come from you. Grant it, O Lord.

How can you begin to imitate Christ in suffering for and with other people?

■ DO NOT BE SURPRISED

1 Peter 4:12-19: "Do not be surprised at the painful trial you are suffering" (v. 12).

The "painful trials" will vary with each of us, but they will come. We are sometimes surprised, even frightened, at how difficult it is to live and act in terms of what we understand to be God's will for our lives. The time will come when we will expect ordeals, and may even learn how to rejoice amidst them.

It is not possible to comprehend the fateful things that happen from time to time. It is not expected that we do, only that we trust God, who in Christ, suffered on our behalf and who will be with us in our trials and conflicts. In addition to trusting God in the midst of trouble, we can cushion its shock and lessen its pain by holding on to one another—by loving, sharing, helping to bear one another's burdens.

This is what it means to belong to the family of God. This is one of our purposes in our representing him in this world. Let us be alert to the needs of one another and help one another to be faithful to God and his purposes. So "do not be surprised at the painful test you are suffering, as though something unusual were happening to you. Rather be glad that you are sharing Christ's sufferings, so that you may be full of joy when his glory is revealed" (TEV).

 I am no longer surprised by the conflicts and troubles that come my way, O Lord. I am still unable to regard them with joy. Yet I do gratefully take comfort in the realization that you are present with me in these painful hours of my life.

Ask God to lead you to the people you need and to those who need you.

◼ COMRADES IN CONFLICT

1 Peter 5:6-11: "The God of all grace . . . after you have suffered . . . will himself restore you and make you strong, firm and steadfast" (v. 10).

Peter urges those of us who are encountering troubles to take heart in the knowledge that we are not alone, that our brothers and sisters throughout the world also have such encounters. We are all sharing in Christ's sufferings. We are comrades in arms in our efforts to resist the Devil and his wiles; we are comrades in conflict as a consequence of our daily battles.

Our responsibilities are enormous, and the risks are many. But we don't have to be afraid for our souls, even if our bodies are exposed to the atrocities of this world. Some of us will fall in battle, but Peter assures us that God himself will restore us and make us strong, firm and steadfast.

"Cast your anxiety on him because he cares for you," wrote Peter. No one will snatch us out of his loving embrace. This is a promise from God. We need to be *aware* lest we fall prey to some adversary that attempts to breach our relationship with God, but we need never be *afraid,* because God truly cares about us. There will be suffering. There is a great God who will give us the grace to endure it—and the courage and wisdom we need to serve him and others through it.

Gracious Father, it is the promise of future restoration and ultimate joy that keeps me plodding in this life. It is the knowledge and witness of my colleagues in the faith that gives me courage. It is the assurance that even if I fall, I shall be reconciled to you.

Reach out to a "comrade in conflict."

■ SHARING THE DIVINE NATURE

2 Peter 1:3-11: "His divine power has given us everything we need . . ." (v. 3).

It is true! Our great and loving God *has* granted through his Spirit everything we need to be happy and productive as his children and servants. Like money in our savings account, however, God's precious gifts are often "on hold," and our spiritual lives remain dwarfed and impoverished, largely dependent on small talents and starved by large doubts. It is not surprising that even petty troubles obscure our spiritual vision and impede our Christian walk.

The problem is with a puny faith. We still haven't learned how to cash in on God's glorious promises, and our lives are consequently less effective or productive. This doesn't have to be. "God's divine power has given us everything we need to live a truly religious life through our knowledge of the one who called us to share in his own glory and goodness" (TEV). He has already given to us these divine gifts that by means of these promises and powers we "participate in the divine nature and escape the corruption [not the *trouble*] in the world caused by evil desires."

He has also given us the wisdom and power to deal with our troubles. We need to respond with faith, kindness, goodness, courage and fortitude, a persistent search for truth, a dogged determination to keep going, a day-by-day surrender to God and his purposes.

 O Lord, if Peter had this kind of faith, why can't I? Thank you for granting me everything I need to overcome or deal with the troubles before me.

Memorize 2 Peter 1:3.

◼ WE ARE GOD'S CHILDREN NOW

1 John 3:1-3: "How great is the love the Father has lavished on us" (v. 1).

We are God's children now! This status or relationship is not something we work or wait for; it is here and now. This is the gift and consequence of God's love. Because of this truth, we nevermore need to question our identity or doubt our significance. We are and always shall be members of the family of God.

When we dare to take this truth seriously, a whole new light emanates from the troubles and trials that besiege us. The problems may remain unsolved, and suffering is still painful, but the fear is removed, and we are given the stamina and courage to go on. There is no suffering or conflict in all the universe that can change our relationship to God. We are God's children now—and forever.

As God's children, however, we can no longer entertain those things that are grievous to our Father. Nor can we dedicate our lives to projects that do not serve him or our fellow beings. As God's children we are expected to relate to God's design for our lives, an exciting, risk-filled style of living that guarantees real freedom and joy, objective and purpose, in the midst of this world's oppression and pain.

"How great is the love the Father has lavished on us!"

I praise you, God, from whom all blessings flow —above all, for the perpetual blessing of your eternal love that establishes me forever as your beloved child. It is this that takes the fear and pain out of many of my troubles.

Affirm today: "How great is the love the Father has lavished on *me*."

◼ GOD'S CHILDREN AND THE EVIL ONE

1 John 5:18-20:   "We know that we belong to God even though the world is under the rule of the Evil One" (v. 19 TEV).

Not God, but the "spiritual hosts of wickedness" are responsible for many of the troubles that we encounter. This does not mean that we must expect some demon or other to be stalking us around every corner. We need to be aware, however, that the Evil One is present and, through temptation and trouble, seeks to woo us away from our Creator and Redeemer. He is active and powerful in our lives and institutions. While the first chapter of Job gives the impression that we are but pawns in the hands of invisible chess players, with God and Satan battling for our souls, the New Testament clearly states that "we belong to God" and he isn't about to allow us to fall into the hands of the Enemy.

God has, nevertheless, entrusted us to a world in which this Enemy is presently in control, and while God does not or cannot always shield us from all the Enemy's attempts to destroy us or lead us astray, he has provided the armor, the weapons, the grace to battle our way through the fierce onslaughts of the Evil One. It is this armor and this grace that we can apply to many of the troubles that afflict us.

"I give them eternal life," said Jesus, "and they shall never perish, and no one can snatch them out of my hand" (John 10:28).

 You entrusted me to a world where evil appears to hold all the cards. But the ultimate victory is with you, great God, so my hope remains alive.

Remind yourself today: "I belong to God. No one can snatch me out of his hands."

■ THE VICTORY IS ASSURED

Rev. 1:9-18: ". . . as a follower of Jesus I am your partner in patiently enduring the suffering that comes to those who belong to his Kingdom" (v. 9 TEV).

While some contemporary prophets regard John's Revelation as a blueprint that spells out what will transpire before the final return of Christ, the primary reason for John's Revelation was to interject hope into the despair of his fellow Christians, who were clinging to their faith against tremendous odds. His brothers and sisters in Christ were facing troubles that make our adversities appear pale and insignificant.

John is also our "partner in patiently enduring the suffering that comes to those who belong to his kingdom." His Revelation gives us the same assurance that he gave to the suffering believers of his day. There is no promise of immediate deliverance from our sufferings. There is, however, the guarantee of ultimate deliverance in John's majestic pictures of the resurrected Christ and the exciting message he has to his followers: "Fear not, I am the first and the last, and the living one; I died, and behold I am alive for evermore."

"Hang in there! Keep the faith!" John is telling us. "These are indeed difficult times for Christians, but the final victory is God's—and it is ours!"

 Thank you, God, for the innumerable saints and soldiers of the faith who are our partners in suffering, and who witnessed to your love and power in their suffering.

Imagine Christ saying to you, "Fear not! The victory is yours."

WHEN TROUBLES WILL BECOME EXTINCT

Rev. 21:1-4: "He will wipe every tear from their eyes" (v. 4).

When all else fails to comfort us in our troubles or blot out the painful memories of illness or sorrow, we can still turn to the blessed promise of a time when all this will pass away. It is that day when Christ will, once and for all, reveal himself as the living, victorious Lord of heaven and earth. Evil will be eradicated— and that means all the troubles that have their source therein. All stumbling blocks, everything that could impede our walk with God, will be removed. Those who oppose God and his people will be put down. Sorrow will turn into joy, darkness will become light, tears will give way to laughter, ugliness will yield to beauty. Wars will cease, and peace shall encompass all peoples.

Words cannot fully describe this fantastic event, but God's faithful children can believe it, hope for it, and anticipate it. All the pain and suffering, trials and tribulations that encompassed us in this world will be forgotten in the glorious revelation of Christ as King. This is the harbinger of hope and comfort John's Revelation offered to the suffering Christians of his day. It continues to offer comfort and hope to each of us today.

"The dwelling of God is with us." Let us celebrate it!

 I do celebrate it, my Lord! The hope that keeps me afloat in the tempest that rages about me is the promise of total union with you, and the dispersion of all my trials and tears on the day of your coming.

Read Revelation 21 and let it fill you with hope.

■ PRAYERS AND PROCLAMATIONS FOR TROUBLED TIMES

I am significant!
But I seldom feel significant.
I was never at the head of my class.
I have never made much money.
I don't expect I will ever earn a doctorate.
My religious training placed a high priority on
    humility and taught me that
        "God chose what is foolish . . . weak . . . low and
        despised . . . things that are not, to bring to nothing
        things that are . . . so that no human being might
        boast."
So it became natural for me to put myself down
    rather than push myself ahead.

As I matured in the faith,
    I learned through counselors and teachers and
    loving friends that I am indeed significant.
It's an eternal truth declared and persistently
    reiterated by God's Word that no sin or failure can
    nullify.
No matter who I am or appear to be,
    whatever my past upbringing or present
    circumstances, my weaknesses or distortions, my
    successes or defeats, I am significant.
I am because of God's creation, Christ's redemption,
    and the gift and indwelling of the Holy Spirit.
This means that I am God's child and Christ's disciple
    and the vessel and vehicle of the Holy Spirit.

It is this that has so much to do with the attitudes
    with which I confront the troubles
    and trials that crowd my path.
They may be painful, or stifling,
    even defeating, embarrassing,
    but I can stand tall and do battle,
    immersed in hope and strength,
    because I am significant.
I may fall in battle,
    but I shall, by the grace of God, rise again,
    because I am important to God.
I am significant.

L ord, you have entrusted us to a rolling ball that
    circles a great sun at the speed of 18 miles each
    second.
No one knows how long this has been going on,
    but since the first man and woman into whom
    you breathed the breath of life and energy,
    there are now almost five billion of your creatures
    on this planet—one of the smallest of the countless
    spheres that move throughout your great universe.
What is so amazing and incomprehensible
    is that you have proclaimed and demonstrated
    love and concern for each one of us on this
    spaceship we call our world.

But what about our world, Lord?
We have, through your gift of freedom and
    individuality,
    and all the other gifts designed
    to sustain and enrich our lives on this world,
    endangered our very existence as well as the earth
    itself, along with her past history and future
    potentialities, by our careless, selfish, evil use of
    these gifts.

This could well be the cause of most of our troubles,
Lord. We seek to be restored to your orbit for
    our lives,
    to be reconciled to your creative purposes and to
    your image bestowed upon us at our creation.

Grant to us, O God of our salvation,
    the wisdom and power to carry on your creative
    activity, and to reach out in love and peace and
    justice to your creatures on this beautiful world.

Your world is so beautiful and bountiful, Lord,
    and we treat it so shabbily.
We have polluted the waters we drink,
    the air we breathe,
    decimated the majestic forests,
    and littered the green hills and valleys with our
        wastes.
Only the mountain peaks we cannot reach,
    the ocean depths we cannot plumb,
    the jungles we cannot penetrate,
    the universal planets and stars we cannot control,
    remain as you created them—
    untouched by the greedy, rebellious, mischievous
    hands of your human creatures.
You have commanded us to continue your evolving
    creation, Lord,
    with the gifts you have imparted to us.
Yet we draw on this earth's energy and sacrifice its
    splendor for our own selfish motives.

There are evil forces about us and within us, Lord.
They obscure your will and purposes and infiltrate and
    possess
    the lives of your creatures
    who have not yielded to your lordship.

We would never have believed it could happen, Lord.
But it has happened.
Your creatures, entrusted to keep your world
    beautiful and bountiful,
    have arrived at that point where the world
    that evolved through millions of years
    can now be utterly destroyed in the matter of hours.

Now we are really in trouble, Lord.
We pray desperately for your intervention in this dark
    madness that has overtaken the human family.

We cry out to be reconciled and restored
    to your will and objectives.
Have mercy on us, O God of love and peace.

There is great tribulation in our world, O Lord.
Some of us are still like spectators in the bleachers
    looking down on the horrors that mangle and
    destroy lives in the arena below us.
But those horrors are now extending to the bleachers,
    and every one of us is in some degree accountable
    for the powers of darkness that are enveloping us
    and threatening to devastate the whole world.

Is the Great Tribulation upon us, Lord?
Is the prophesied Armageddon about to explode in
    our faces?
As incredible as it seems,
    some of your children are actually waiting for it,
    even encouraging it to happen,
    assuming that you will snatch them from its
    obliterating power and transport them to your
    kingdom in the skies.
Others of us are desperately seeking for ways to
    hold it back,
    to keep our world and its creatures alive
    until you have fulfilled your purposes
    for us on this globe.

What else can we do, Lord? What would you
    have us to do?
The Armageddon cannot possibly be your doing, Lord.
If and when a nuclear Armageddon takes place,
    it is because your creatures have brought it on
        themselves.

Our Loving God, prepare us for and sustain us
    in whatever tribulations that come our way.
Help us to be clear of mind and loving of heart,
    and to possess the wisdom and courage to carry out
    your purposes and to communicate your saving
        grace
    to our sisters and brothers in the human family
        about us.

Y our father . . . killed at noon today . . . automobile
    accident!"
The terse announcement came from two thousand
    miles away.
It hit like a sharp blow to the belly,
    and left me stunned, gasping for breath.
Then followed the agony of slow, painful realization:
    dad's gone!

I had always known the shadow of death would
eventually
    haunt my hallowed circle,
    but never like this—
    the ugly, grotesque manner of his exit from this life.
It was as if some outlandish nightmare had numbed
    the senses with a dread horror conceived by the
        devil himself.
But the shock gradually focused into reality;
    and the naked fact and manner of dad's passing
    remained unchanged.

I could not accept the traditional "it-was-God's-will"
    response.
God just doesn't do things that way.
I don't know if the devil had anything to do with it.
A careless driver,
    possibly some carelessness on the part of dad
        himself,
    resulted in the crushing death of someone I
        dearly loved.
It was something that even a loving God could
    not prevent.
It had happened; I had to accept it—and move on.

Through the terrible hurt seeps the healing of heaven.
Whatever Satan's insidious intent,
    I was convinced that God was with dad in that
        fateful moment,
    transforming that which was ugly and evil
    into an agent of his eternal purposes.
Dad was promoted from the incompleteness of this
    existence into the fulness and totality of
    God's presence.

The pain remains.
    Alongside of it is peace—and the compulsion to plod
    on, serving the God my father loved and served.

You never said it would be easy, Lord,
    our sojourn in this uncertain, pain-ridden world.
It wasn't easy for you.
You stood firm against Satan's temptations to win over
    the masses with cheap tricks and transcendent
        powers.

You wept bitterly over the death of a dear friend.
You were depressed by the hardness of heart and the
rebelliousness of your people who crowded
about you.
You faced daily and dealt patiently with your feeble,
fickle, slow-learning disciples.
You did not resist the actions of the religious leaders
and their plans to destroy you.

Nor is it easy for us, Lord,
this road we traverse in our determination to
follow you.
You have commanded us to take up our cross, to deny
ourselves,
to risk our lives in service to others.
Sometimes we think you expect too much of us,
our Lord.
We cannot measure up to your high standards.
We continue to fumble and fail,
to flounder about like fish out of water.
We are frightened by the evil forces that contend
with us,
depressed by our many defeats in trying to carry
out your purposes,
dismayed over the obstacles that impede our walk.

Yet we need not doubt your saving, redeeming love,
our Lord.
The same Spirit that worked in and through you
is the Spirit that works in and through our lives.
We praise you, our God:
that we will always be your children, your property,
your very own for all eternity,
that nothing can take us from you,
whatever our troubles and trials,
the sufferings and sorrows that come upon us.

Thank you, O God,
   for the troubles that have come my way.
I know you didn't send them,
   yet I recognize in retrospect that you know about
   them and were present with me to help me deal
      with them.

I thank you that they didn't separate me from you.
I remember fearing at the time that they might
   come between you and me.
I doubted your love for me,
   even your very existence.
I ate of bread that was not the Bread of life;
   I drank from other fountains than that river
   of grace that issues forth from you.
My soul was famished, my throat parched,
   my life embittered as I felt you were edging away
      from me.
I was the one who was off course, out of orbit,
   running down blind allies into dead-end streets.
If only I had paused to listen,
   I would have heard your footsteps behind me,
   following, pursuing, never letting me out of
      your sight.
You were faithful to me, my Lord,
   even as my faith faltered.
I began to sense your concern for me.
Through the love of a friend,
   the written words of your prophets and apostles,
      the proclamations of the Word,
   a great choral anthem,
   I heard your loving entreaty to stop running,
   to still my anxious heart,
   and to trust you in the middle of my black night.
I am grateful, my God, that I am closer to you
   and you are more real to me,
   than ever before.
So I thank you for the troubles that have come
my way.

There is much to rejoice about—
    even in a world of discord and trouble,
    misery and frustration, pain and suffering.
The clouds are so heavy for much of each day,
    but there are bright flashes of light
    that break through to give hope to fainting hearts
    and strength to weak knees.
The fragile flower in all its beauty,
    the oceans in their fury,
    the heavenly bodies glimmering through the
      darkness,
    the magnificent redwoods standing tall and firm
    through centuries of heat and cold and wind,
    all give evidence of the majestic power and splendor
    of our eternal God.
The technological advances that awe and amaze us,
    and even those created out of the energies that
    God made available to us,
    are little more than children's toys when compared
    to the bountiful creation of our Lord.

And what about the courageous spirits of God's
    creatures, noble men and women who have endured
    sufferings more severe than most of us can even
    imagine?
They emerge from their sufferings,
    or live with them,
    like inextinguishable fires that light and warm
    the frigid darkness that encompasses us.
Their very miseries, the crosses they have had to bear,
    have made them tempered vessels of love and peace
    to be poured out upon the human family about
    them.
There is indeed much to rejoice about—
    even in a world subject to nature's calamities
    and its creatures' sin and greed.
Let us celebrate,
    and commit anew our lives and energies
    to serving our loving Creator and God!

There are times, O Lord,
  when our obedience to you and your purposes
  will lead us into trouble.
Your call to take up our cross and follow you
  never promised a comfortable, trouble-free
  existence.
Most of your initial followers were martyred because
  they refused to bow down to unjust laws and
  regulations.
Thousands of your children have been persecuted
  and imprisoned because they placed allegiance to
  you and your absolutes above the laws of men
  who governed them.
You brought down trouble upon your own head
  when you, knowing well it would lead to your
  crucifixion, broke civil and sacred laws by cleansing
  the temple and healing on the Sabbath,
  or protested against the unjust and unloving
  standards of the religious and political leaders.
The saints of Bible history,
  and your followers from the New Testament until
  now, have often found that their allegiance to you
  and to your creatures
  made it necessary for them to defy political
  authorities in scorn of consequences.
Paul wrote much of the Scriptures from a prison cell.
Young men have been disgraced and jailed for
  refusing to take up arms against their fellowmen.
Groups of your children defied their government
  and risked and suffered death in their attempts
  to shield the Jews from Hitler's odious intentions.
How else could the elimination of slavery,
  the pursuit of civil rights,
  the expansion of your kingdom within antireligious
  governments, be accomplished save through those
  willing to risk the troubles and consequences
  of following you rather than Caesar?

Even in this hour,
    there are scores of your children embarking on
    unpopular, even illegal, activities in their attempt
    to stop the arms' race
    and save our world's millions from nuclear
    annihilation.

There are times when we will have to serve you
    and your creatures in the face of trouble, Lord.
Grant us the wisdom and grace and strength and
    courage to serve you well.

I know there are some troubles I must endure, Lord.
There are others I can confront and cope with
    only with your grace.
Yet many of the trials and conflicts that come my way,
    I have brought upon myself.

I have received your gift of salvation, my God.
I know that I am an object of your love.
I believe that you abide in me even as I abide in you.
While you have never failed me,
    there were many times when I have failed you.
I have hurt people by my arrogance,
    offended them in my foolishness.
I have been childish rather than wise,
    proud when I should have been humble,
    indiscreet when I was expected to be prudent.
O Lord, my self-centeredness and my impatience with
    people, my incessant reaching out for tangible joys
    and material security,
    the doubts that rise to obscure my relationship to
    you, have been the cause for many of the troubles
    in my life.
It seems at times that I have matured so little
    in my relationship to you and in my love for others.

I praise you, O Lord,
  because you never give up
  on your faltering, foolish children.
Even while you must allow us to tangle with the
  troubles that we bring upon ourselves,
    you stand ready to forgive us and draw us back into
    your loving embrace.
How patient and gentle you are, O Lord!
Grant to us the grace to become what you would
  have us to be.

p46

p99

peace in adversity (anxiety)   p53 ✳

seeing God in troubled times   p73 ✳

Death   p70

A Real a Loving God —
remember His closeness
a time when He was
very real to you   p71